BILINGUAL AND TRILINGUAL PARENTING 101

A Practical Handbook for Multilingual Families

GW00481277

Ka Yee Meck

FIRST EDITION

www.multilingualfamilyhub.com

Cover design by Elisa Pinizzotto

(Elisapinizzotto at Fiverr.com)

TABLE OF CONTENTS

INTRODUCTION AND HOW TO USE THIS BOOK

First of all, thank you so much for choosing this book. There is certainly no shortage of books on the subject of bilingualism, and a virtually unlimited amount of information on the subject is at the reader's disposal at the click of a button on Google. So why do we need another book on how to raise multilingual children?

This **compact, no-nonsense handbook** has been specifically created for busy modern parents, who don't have the time to scour through the vast existing literature and online information. If you're looking for **a step-by-step guide on how to activate your child's linguistic ability**, as well as **practical tips and advice that you can put into practice today**, I am confident that this book is just what you need. Essentially, I have done all the reading and research so you don't have to!

Aside from general tips and advice on how to raise bilingual / trilingual children, I will also share with you a highly effective method for tackling an extremely common problem: your child can understand the target language, but always replies to you in English (or whatever language is dominant where you live). To my knowledge, this is the only book on the market that targets this specific problem.

I have deliberately kept this book light on academic theory but you will find all the necessary references in the endnotes section; while I've kept technical jargon to a minimum, a glossary section has been included that explains any technical terms used throughout this book.

Just as importantly, this book was written from a parent's perspective. It's truly a book created *for* parents, *by* a real-life parent. While I don't have a PhD in Linguistics, I *am* a mum-of-two who is actively (and successfully, if I say so myself!) raising her own children to be fluent in three languages. As such, **I will only share with you techniques that I have used and would use with my own children; techniques that *anyone* could implement in real life.**

Besides my parenting "credentials", I also have a decade of professional experience in translation and language teaching – language learning and teaching is both my passion and my bread and butter. Through this book and my website (www.multilingualfamilyhub.com), **my one overriding goal is to help other families out there who want to raise bilingual, trilingual and multilingual children, and reap all the benefits that being fluent in more than one language brings**.

I truly believe that anyone can successfully help their child become bilingual or trilingual. All you need is determination, perseverance, and the right tools and method. My husband and I were so close to abandoning our goal of raising our kids to be trilingual, as the obstacles just seemed too great. I will share with you the story of how we overcame these obstacles.   If we can do it, so can you!

Welcome on board this amazing journey – yes, it will almost certainly be a bumpy ride, and at times you may want to tear your hair out, scream in frustration and even be tempted to throw in the towel altogether, *but* I promise you – **as long as you don't give up, and hopefully with the help of this book, *you will get there*.** And the tremendous rewards both for you and your child will be worth all the effort a hundred times over!

So, are you ready to help your child achieve their language potential, discover the beauty and wonders of languages, and reap all the benefits of being fluent in more than one language?

Let's go!

How to use this book

This book was conceived as a practical how-to guide that's easy for readers to dip in and out of.

If you're still expecting your first child, or if you're in the very early stages of your bilingual/ multilingual journey, it's a good idea to simply read this book in the order it's written to get an overview of everything. Feel free to skip over any sections that are not relevant to you at this stage – you can always come back to them later.

If you specifically want to find out how to help your child make that transition from understanding the target language (see Glossary in the Appendix) but not speaking it, to actively speaking the target language, feel free to skip straight to Chapter 6. In that chapter, I will guide you through step-by-step what I've called "The Bootcamp Method", an intensive "training programme" that has been specifically developed to tackle this very common and often tricky issue.

Chapter 7 is structured like an "FAQ" section, answering some common questions parents may have when it comes to raising multilingual children.

For inspiration, activity ideas and resources, check out Chapters 8 and 9. Everything is bullet-pointed for easy reference.

Please note:

1. In English there's always this pesky little issue of "gender" when deciding which personal pronoun to use for a word like "child". For the sake of simplicity, I will use the plural forms ("they", "them" and "their") throughout this book.
2. All the "case studies" in this book are 100% based on people I know in real life. To protect their privacy, all names have

been changed. On the other hand, "examples" are hypothetical and are not based on real people I know.

3. I try to avoid technical jargon as much as possible but it's difficult to write a book like this without the occasional references to technical terms. Please see the Glossary section for a quick explanation of some of the key terms used throughout this book.

4. Throughout this book, I will use the words "Chinese" and "Mandarin" interchangeably. The word "Cantonese" will be used to refer to the Cantonese dialect specifically.

CHAPTER 1

MY FAMILY'S LANGUAGE JOURNEY

This is *not* a book about my family and me so I'll only share with you what's relevant. This chapter will be a brief summary of the journey my husband and I have undertaken in raising our kids to be trilingual, and how we overcame the "my-kid-will-only-speak-to-me-in-English" problem.

In September 2016, I became a first-time mum to my son, Alexey. Even before he was born, my husband and I already started thinking about which languages we should speak to him in.

I was born in Shanghai, China, before moving to Hong Kong as a toddler. My mother was born and raised in Shanghai; her mother tongue is the Shanghainese dialect but she's also fluent in Mandarin as well as Cantonese (and now English too).

Having spent most of my childhood in the British colony, I consider my mother tongue to be Cantonese, but due to my family connections I am also fluent in Mandarin, and have been working as a translator and Mandarin language instructor for a decade. Although my mother's mother tongue is Shanghainese, she never used the language at home with us probably because my father did not speak the language. It's something I mildly regret – Shanghai natives are a famously proud bunch and they don't always remember (or bother) to switch to Mandarin for my benefit!

To make things more complicated though, I've lived in the UK since the age of seventeen. Having spent more than half of my life and all my adult life in the UK, I consider myself to be perfectly fluent in

English. In terms of literacy skills and vocabulary size, English is certainly my strongest language. In fact, in most everyday as well as professional situations, I feel most comfortable in English, so to all intents and purposes English is now my dominant language.

My husband was born in Russia in the late 1970s before emigrating to Australia as a teenager. He considers Russian to be his mother tongue, although like me, his dominant language is now probably English, due to having lived in English-speaking countries (first Australia, then the UK) for three decades.

For him it was an easy decision – he would speak to our son in Russian, but not only that, he also wanted me to speak Russian when the three of us were interacting together, which was a pretty daunting prospect for me as my command of Russian was (and still is) very basic.

Before Alexey was born, I couldn't decide if I should speak to him in Cantonese (a Chinese dialect spoken in Hong Kong and the Canton/Guangdong region of China) or Mandarin (the official language of China). In fact, I think the first few days after he was born, I just spoke to him in English – my brain was a total mush in those early days and all grand plans I had about raising a trilingual kid were all but forgotten in a sleep-deprived fog. But gradually, speaking to him in Cantonese came naturally to me, and that's the language I used with him for the first two years of his life.

Alexey started speaking a bit later than his monolingual peers but his development was still well within the normal range. At age two, he had a vocabulary of about 50 words, most of which were English, the rest a mix of Cantonese and Russian words. He understood all three languages very well. When he was 19 months old, his little sister Alina was born, and I also spoke to her in Cantonese.

My husband and I always knew that we wanted our kids to learn Mandarin because it's a much more widely-spoken language and therefore arguably more "useful" than Cantonese. But to begin with, we thought three languages were enough to start with so Mandarin was "put on hold", so to speak. However, around the time Alexey turned two, I had an informal chat with a language specialist at our local children's centre, who said that there was no reason not to introduce Mandarin now if we planned to do it at some point anyway. So at this point, my husband and I made a conscious decision to add Mandarin to our household language mix. In reality, I soon began to use Mandarin exclusively with the children and gradually dropped Cantonese, as I found it difficult to keep two languages going in parallel. With the knowledge I have now, I probably would've done things differently – it certainly *is* possible to raise quadrilingual children and I'll offer suggestions on how to do that later in this book.

When I first introduced Mandarin, Alexey did seem somewhat confused, but to my relief, he picked up the new language very quickly, at least in terms of passive understanding. By age three, he understood everything that my mother or I said to him in Mandarin, and he could say approximately 10 words and phrases. Yet, despite relatively good progress, whenever my husband or I talked to him in our respective languages, Alexey would *always* reply in English.

At the time I thought this was quite normal – and it *is*, of course. In my experience talking to other multilingual families, this seems to be a very common scenario. "My child understands everything I say," the mum would tell me, "but he always answers in English. What can you do?"

At that time, my husband and I kind of just accepted the situation for what it was – that Alexey could understand Russian and Mandarin but not speak them. Well, I thought, that's still better than nothing. If he wants to pick it up later, he can, surely – or so I reasoned to myself.

One day I was at our local children's centre when an Albanian nanny commented on how I was reading a book with my kids in Chinese. We were looking at pictures of animals in a book. I would say the animal name in Chinese, and the kids would point at the correct picture. And here I was, feeling pretty proud of myself and even a bit smug! But the Albanian lady said, why don't you teach them to say the words in Chinese? "Pointing is easy," she said, "anyone can do it!"

To be totally honest, I was quite taken aback by her comment and felt somewhat defensive. I explained that Alexey understood Chinese perfectly, but would only speak in English. She wasn't being rude at all but genuinely wanted to give me some helpful advice. Her own children, she told me, were fully bilingual and biliterate (see Glossary) in both English and Albanian. She went on to tell me that the family she worked for was also very strict about making the kids speak the parents' languages (Swedish and German). So strict, in fact, that the Albanian nanny had never heard the mum say *a single word* of English in the children's presence, ever, not even a simple word like "no"! Her point was that it *can* be done.

That really got me thinking – maybe I am not trying hard enough? *Were my husband and I just taking the path of least resistance?* Was it just wishful thinking on our part to think that one day, *if* and *when* they want to, they can just pick things up easily and start speaking the languages effortlessly?

The Turning Point

Everything changed on a typically grey autumn day in London, November 2019. We were at a friends' birthday party when I started chatting to Guy (name has been changed), a French-speaking dad. He was married to a New Zealander and their two beautiful daughters were fully bilingual in English and French. I explained our situation to him, and the advice he gave me that day – at risk of sounding a wee bit dramatic – really changed our lives. And his advice formed the basis on which I later developed "The Bootcamp Method".

Firstly, he said, **it's really important that you should speak to your child in your language most of the time, even in other people's**

company. At this point, I wasn't very consistent in speaking Mandarin all the time with my children. I would guess that approximately 20-30% of the time I would switch to English, mostly because I felt rude and awkward speaking Chinese to the kids when there were other people around. But Guy said that in London at least, no one would care! And when I really thought about it, I realised that even when I was alone with the children, I sometimes just switched to English for no apparent reason – I wasn't even *aware* that I was doing it, until I really reflected on it. In retrospect, I probably did it because Alexey always talked to me in English so it sometimes felt more natural to reply to him in English. So the first thing I had to do was to be more consistent in using the target language.

The other crucial piece of advice he gave me was this**: every time they say something in English, make them say it again in your target language. EVERY. SINGLE. TIME.** It's so simple, yet over time I realised just how powerful this deceptively obvious technique is. It is, by far, the single most important thing I did which helped Alexey made that seemingly impossible leap from passive understanding to active speaking.

Anyway, during our conversation, I was intrigued but also daunted by the prospect of having to do something that seemed so… *drastic*! And at this point, Alexey spoke almost *zero* Mandarin – was this really going to work? How long would it take before I saw results?

Guy said it would most likely take a few months but it *would* work, if I persevered. Something he said really stuck with me – as their mother or father, you are the centre of your child's world. If they *have* to speak the target language to communicate with you, they will. You have to create the *need* and *motivation* for them to use the target language.

He also told me about his own family background – he was born in France to Dutch parents, but for some reason they never taught him to speak Dutch, probably because they lived in a small rural town and the parents were more concerned about assimilation than passing on their language to the next generation. Guy said that this was something that he'd always regretted – he felt that his parents sometimes struggled to communicate their most deeply felt feelings to him because French wasn't their mother tongue after all. This echoes the sentiments of virtually every one else I've spoken to who's been in a similar situation. So many of my friends and acquaintances have told me, "I wish my parents had spoken to me in Chinese/ Vietnamese/ French…" Making an effort to pass on your language to your child can help preempt such regrets.

Another thing he said that really resonated with me was this: **"If you don't do it, no one else will. It's you and your child against the world!"** And I thought – this is so true! We're not in a position to send our kids to a bilingual school, nor do we have a lot of Mandarin-speaking friends and family here. And in the middle of a global pandemic (at the time of writing), it's not like we can just jet off to Shanghai to spend the summer with my extended family there with the kids, which *would* be the best way to give them a proper immersive learning environment. If I don't put in the work, who will? And dear reader – no one in the world cares more about your child's education and development more than *you* do. *Do this not for yourself, but for your child.* As parents, we would all move mountains for our kids. And while trying to raise a bilingual/ multilingual child is undeniably hard work, it is something that millions of parents around the world have achieved so simply saying "it's too hard!" really isn't a valid excuse!

Now, back to the story. This serendipitous encounter with a fellow parent really gave me the motivation needed to up my game. In fact, I put his advice into practice the very same day, on our way home from Marylebone to West Hampstead. I still remember our journey home on the 139 bus that day, me speaking Mandarin to Alexey, him replying in English, and me coaxing him to repeat everything in Mandarin… It didn't help that there were a couple of Chinese students sitting just across the aisle from us watching us in mild amusement. You might find yourself in a similar situation one day but just remember, you'll never see these people again whereas your child's language skills will (hopefully) stay with them forever!

Fast forward a year and a half, both Alexey (aged 4 years and 10 months at the time of writing) and his sister Alina (3 years and 3 months) are fluent in Mandarin, Russian and English in varying degrees. In fact, after I started implementing Guy's advice (which I formulated into "The Bootcamp Method" in this book – see Chapter 6) in November 2019, by February 2020 Alexey had already achieved fluency in Chinese. I remember this milestone very clearly because it was around this time when my Chinese cousin, who lives in Berlin, visited us; she was impressed by Alexey's fluency in Mandarin and was inspired to do the same with her half-German son, Oskar. So in short, **it only took about *three months* for us to see concrete results.**

Funnily enough, almost exactly a year later to the day, in November 2020, I bumped into Guy at a park in London. I told him how our little chat a year ago had made such a huge difference to our children's linguistic abilities. He was really pleased for us. I told my husband about this chance encounter that same evening; looking back, we couldn't believe that merely twelve months ago, Alexey *only* spoke English and now, merely twelve months later, he spoke *three* languages, albeit imperfectly. Our experience is real-life proof of how daily incremental changes can add up to something genuinely life-changing in as little as one year. Had we not done something about it, a year would have passed just as quickly and nothing – or very little – would've changed in terms of Alexey's ability to speak Mandarin and Russian.

I could be wrong – maybe he would have started speaking these languages of his own accord without our intervention although, to be totally honest, I highly doubt it. Based on my own observation of other families, if a child doesn't speak the parents' language(s) by about three or four, they are very unlikely to start speaking it later on without some intervention or a drastic change in their linguistic environment (e.g. moving to a different country), especially if they start spending more time at nursery or pre-school. I will explain the reasons for this later in this book.

A "bonus" benefit of our effort was that our second child, Alina, had a much, much smoother path to being trilingual. She started speaking in all three languages from the very early days, and we never had to train her intensively to get her to speak Russian and Chinese. Of course, it might just be a combination of her being female (when it comes to linguistic and communication skills, girls are known to develop at a faster pace than boys in early childhood)[i], a second child (children with older siblings are known to be more advanced in their development in early childhood)[ii], and her own individual abilities. But it's also highly possible that having an older brother as a trilingual role model made it much easier for her to do the same from an early age.

All this might not have happened were it not for the advice Guy gave me on that day back in 2019. For this I will always be grateful. And in this book, I'd like to share with you "The Bootcamp Method", and everything else I've learnt about raising multilingual kids along the way so far. Just as Guy has helped me, parent-to-parent, I hope to help you and your family achieve your goals too.

In the next chapter, let's take a quick look at the wonderful benefits of being fluent in more than one language.

CHAPTER 2

THE BENEFITS OF SPEAKING MORE THAN ONE LANGUAGE

Before we get to the nuts-and-bolts of how to raise multilingual kids, I'd like to talk about the benefits of being fluent in more than one language. Even if you're already fully convinced of the benefits of bilingualism or multilingualism, you may still find some useful or interesting facts in this section. Raising multilingual kids can be hard work – keeping these benefits in mind will hopefully help you stay motivated and focused!

1. Communicate with family members/ extended family and friends

This point probably applies to a significant proportion of parents who want to raise their children to be bilingual or multilingual. While you and your partner are most likely fluent in English (or whichever majority language is applicable to your family), you might have relatives back home who don't speak English; wouldn't it be a pity if your kids couldn't talk to their own grandparents or cousins back home?

My mother told me about a Chinese friend of hers who's lived in the UK for more than 20 years but speaks very little English. Yet somewhat surprisingly, she never taught her daughter to speak Chinese either. A few years ago my mother's friend became really ill, and due to her lack of English, needed her daughter to assist with visits to the hospital and other tasks. The mum ended up having to use a dictionary to communicate with her own daughter, and it was at this point that the realisation really hit home – she had sadly missed the opportunity to pass on her language to her own child, an opportunity she would never have again. A Vietnamese-Australian friend of mine also laments the fact that he can't discuss anything more profound than what's for dinner with his own parents, due to the language barrier.

These are obviously extreme examples but they really serve to **highlight the most basic function of language – it is ultimately a tool with which to communicate with another human being, and to build meaningful relationships**. There's no better reason to learn a language than to be able to speak to a loved one, and to connect to your heritage, which brings us to the next point.

2. Connect to your heritage and cultural identity

Having a hybrid heritage can be a wonderful thing. We live in a world that increasingly celebrates diversity and embraces the richness of all cultures. However, the flip side is that **children who do have a heritage – or even two or more heritages – that is different from the dominant culture can sometimes struggle to find their own identity. And being bilingual/ trilingual can really help one feel more secure in one's identity/ identities.**

I've read countless interviews where people who come from "immigrant" backgrounds have expressed this sentiment, but one that I've read recently particularly resonated with me. I stumbled upon this article while reading up on the Backstreet Boys (as you do!); it's a fascinating read if you're interested in how mixed-heritage children can struggle with their own identities[iii].

One of the five members of the group, Howie Dorough, was born to a Puerto Rican mother and an Irish-American father. In the interview, he said that there were times that he'd be in situations around other

Puerto Ricans or Hispanics and they'd start speaking in Spanish, and he'd be looking at them going "*No halo español!*" ("I don't speak Spanish!") "As I started getting older, I definitely felt challenged with finding my identity," said Dorough. His inability to speak Spanish also had a significant impact on his career: "I realized I was limited by not being able to embrace that side of me, especially in the entertainment world." But in his later years he took Spanish classes and achieved a good level of fluency. "It's not the best Spanish – it's all the present tense […] but I've been able to embrace it now and feel more secure with my culture."

Being a mother of two mixed-heritage kids, Dorough's experience feels very relevant and instructive. My husband and I hope to give our children the best chance of learning Chinese and Russian well enough to connect to their parental heritages, if they should wish. **Our view is that parents should, where possible, empower their children with these tools; it's then up to the children what to do with them.**

3. Gain more in-depth understanding of other cultures

This point is closely linked to point two. Just as language is indispensable for connecting to one's heritage, a people's culture is also inextricably linked to its language. **If you want to know a culture in any depth, you really need to get to grips with the language that's associated with that culture and/or people; without that knowledge, no matter how many times you visit a place, it will be virtually impossible to move beyond a "Disneyland" cultural experience and a tourist's perspective.** How can it be otherwise, if you don't have a clue what the locals are saying to one another, no idea what any of the TV shows are talking about?

In the case of my own family, although most of our extended family members on both my and my husband's side speak good English, we would still love to enable our kids to learn more about the cultures of their forebears by raising them to be trilingual. And when they do visit their parents' native countries one day, they will hopefully gain more cultural insight than the average tourist and feel empowered to engage with the culture and people in a more meaningful way.

Not only does being fluent in another language help you navigate other cultures; on a practical level, it also enables you to communicate with a bigger part of humanity. Knowing the Chinese language, for example, enables you to communicate with *1.4 billion more people*. Sure, an increasing number of people in China and elsewhere are proficient in English to some extent. But as the quote (usually attributed to Nelson Mandela) sums it up beautifully: *"If you talk to a man in a language he understands, that goes to his head. If you talk to him in his own language, that goes to his heart."*

Quite apart from any practical benefits, **being bilingual or multilingual is simply an enriching experience in its own right.** If you could give them the gift of language from a young age that will enable them to unlock this wonderful wealth of experience over a lifetime, why throw this opportunity away?

4. Broaden children's horizons and help them become "global citizens"

The pros and cons of globalisation are clearly beyond the scope of this book. Nevertheless, if you're reading this book, I hope it's not too presumptuous to assume that you and your family probably have a somewhat international outlook. It has often been observed that being bilingual or multilingual seems to make people more open-minded. **Learning a language has a way of opening the mind up to different perspectives and ways of looking at the world, making a person more receptive to the views of others**. I'm sure this is a quality that most parents would love their child to have.

My husband and I, along with our two children, were lucky enough to live in a very multicultural, cosmopolitan part of London up until fairly recently. We've now moved to Hertfordshire just outside London, but we still have lots of friends from all over the world, many of whom are raising their children to be bilingual or trilingual too. Because Alexey and Alina now speak Chinese and Russian, in addition to English, they are very aware of the existence of other languages and cultures. We'd often look at a world map together and talk about our friends and extended families – "Look, this is Colombia, where Eva's daddy is from"; "Do you remember which of your friends is from Mongolia?" One of my fondest memories of the apartment block where we used to live in West Hampstead, was when my neighbours' children and my kids were looking at a tree together in the communal garden, and I asked each of them how to say "leaf" in their family's language. "*Feuille!*" (French)! "*Hoja!*" (Spanish) "*Shuye!*" (Chinese) – came the chorus of reply, from this wonderful group of little polyglots!

Of course, you could still help your children develop cultural awareness as a monolingual family; in no way am I suggesting that monolingual people are inherently less culturally aware. But there is no denying that speaking more than one language does help people see things from a different perspective, which can only be a good thing.

5. Give your kid's brain a boost (it's scientifically proven, and it's free!)

In this day and age, there always seems to be a new product that promises to elevate your child to the status of baby Einstein. I once read about a mum who "trained" her newborn baby (as in, literally, one-day-old) with phonics flashcards, in the hope of giving the baby a head start in the race that is modern life. Such examples abound.

Now, I'm not saying that being bilingual will make your child a genius, or even more intelligent – if that was the case, all kids from, say Malaysia (or any other country where multilingualism is actually the norm), would be busy making space shuttles or inventing the latest cancer cure. **It's actually really important to remember that** *around the world, more than half of people –between 60-75%* **according to studies cited by the BBC**[iv] *– speak more than one* *language.* This is both humbling and liberating; humbling because so many people around the world can effortlessly accomplish something that can seem so unachievable to those from a monolingual background, and liberating because if so many people around the world can do it naturally, it's actually *not such a big deal*, and there's absolutely no reason why your child, or in fact any other average human being, cannot do it! In the Anglophone world, bilingualism/ multilingualism is so often worshipped on a pedestal, something to be admired in awe, but really, it's time to tear it down from that pedestal and bring it back down to earth. We need to demystify bilingualism/ multilingualism, and re-establish it as something that's actually very *normal*.

Nevertheless, there is solid scientific evidence which shows that knowing more than one language is beneficial for cognitive and executive functions of the brain, as bilinguals and multilingual have to constantly juggle two or more systems in their heads. According to cognitive neuropsychologist Jubin Abutalebi, *it is possible to* *distinguish bilingual people from monolinguals simply by looking at* *scans of their brains*, as bilinguals have significantly more grey matter than monolinguals in their anterior cingulate cortex, because they are using it so much more often[v]. Now, I don't know about you, but I find this pretty staggering – that being bilingual or multilingual actually alters your brain structure in an objectively measureable way!

In recent years the effect of bilingualism on dementia and Alzheimer's disease has also come to the forefront of public consciousness. While being bilingual doesn't prevent people from getting dementia, **numerous studies indicate that it can delay its onset by an average of five years[vi].** If a "magic pill" were to have the same effect, thereby hugely improving people's quality of life over an extended period of time, be in no doubt that all the big pharmaceutical companies would start a fierce bidding war over it! And one can only imagine how much such a "magic pill" would cost...

And yet, *you* could give your child this gift *for free*. When you look at it this way, isn't it a bit crazy not to raise your child with more than one language if you're in the position to do so?

6. Help your child gain a competitive edge in the future job market

This benefit is pretty self-explanatory. I could be slightly biased, since my work as a translator and language tutor literally revolves around languages, but **various recent surveys show that being multilingual can improve one's earning potential by anything from 3% to as much as 15%,** by some estimates[vii]. Bilingual and multilingual candidates are also more likely to be hired in the first place.

Does this surprise anyone? Say you were an employer, and there were two potential candidates going for the same job. All things being equal, would you not favour the candidate who speaks three languages, as opposed to just one? And in our increasingly inter-connected world, fluency in more than one language will become an even more valuable asset.

It is true that artificial intelligence will drastically improve the efficacy and accuracy of translation software such as Google Translate, to the point where many sceptics already question the value and purpose of learning another language – what's the point if a computer can do the translation for you instantaneously, even in face-to-face interactions with a real person, as envisaged by some?

But in reality, we are probably still a long way off from that. For 99.99% of our existence as a species, we *Homo Sapiens* have evolved to interact face-to-face, using natural language. Such deeply hard-wired instincts and preferences will not be so easily displaced by technology. **As long as we're still flesh-and-blood human beings, the ability to converse naturally in another language will continue to be an extremely valuable skill.**

Many parents make huge sacrifices to give their children an expensive education, in the hope that it will give them a head start in life. So if you could give your child's future career prospects a boost simply by raising them to speak more than one language, and do so for free, is there any legitimate reason not to do it?

7. Being bilingual makes it easier to learn additional languages

Several parents have told me that they don't see the point of raising their kids to be bilingual, as their languages are too "niche" and are quite frankly not very "useful", so it's hardly worth the effort.

While this pragmatic viewpoint is understandable, these parents might have overlooked one important benefit of being bilingual – studies have shown that **being fluent in a second language makes it easier to learn additional languages.** In one fascinating study conducted by Professors Salim Abu-Rabia and Ekaterina Sanitsky of the Department of Special Education at the University of Haifa[viii], two groups of 6th grade students in Israel were chosen to represent a sample of students studying English as a foreign language. The first group comprised 40 students, who were immigrants from the former Soviet Union states, whose mother tongue was Russian and who spoke fluent Hebrew as a second language. The second group comprised 42 native Hebrew-speaking students with no fluency in another language. The first group was given tests in Russian, Hebrew and English, while the second group was given tests in Hebrew and English only.

After comparing the results of these tests, the researchers were able to conclude that those students whose mother tongue was Russian demonstrated higher proficiency not only in the new language (English), but also in Hebrew. The scholars noted that the fact that the Russian speakers had better Hebrew skills than the native Hebrew speakers themselves indicates that acquiring a mother tongue and preserving that language in a bilingual environment is not detrimental to acquiring a second language – on the contrary, **fluency and skills in one language are beneficial for the acquisition of a second language, and possessing skills in two languages can boost the learning process of a third language. "This is because languages reinforce one another, and provide tools to strengthen phonologic, morphologic and syntactic skills,"** Professor Abu-Rabi explains.

So even if you think your language is of little practical or commercial value in the wider world, raising your child to be bilingual will equip them with the linguistic and cognitive skills to learn more "useful" languages in the future. Why deprive them of this advantage? Besides, in today's unpredictable world, a not-so-useful language today could become much more valuable in 20 years' time – you just never know. An Australian-Chinese friend of mine, who resented having to go to Chinese school when she was little, spoke of her experience: "30 years ago, who would have thought that China would become the next superpower?" Now she wishes she'd taken her Sunday classes more seriously!

I hope this chapter has given you some food for thought and a motivational boost. You're in it for the long haul so on those days when you want to throw that workbook out the window, when you feel like giving up, when you'd rather watch funny cat videos on Youtube for 15 minutes than sit through another homework session with your child – remember that those efforts are, at the end of the day, *so* worth it. And be assured that when your child grows up, they will be grateful for the wonderful gift of language you've worked so hard to bestow on them.

In the next chapter, I will set out the "Seven Key Principles", which will to a large extent determine the success of your endeavor to raise multilingual children.

CHAPTER 3

THE SEVEN KEY PRINCIPLES

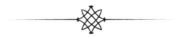

No matter which strategy (see Chapter 4 for the "Big Three" Strategies) you choose to adopt, or what stage you're currently at, the seven key principles I've outlined below are essential to helping your child become fluent in the target language. Let me take you through them one by one.

1. The golden equation: BILINGUAL SUCCESS = EXPOSURE + NEED

If you take away only *one* thing from this book, let it be this: when you strip everything down, bilingual/ multilingual success ultimately depends on two conditions being met sufficiently: **EXPOSURE** to the target language, and creating the **NEED** to speak the language.

This is it. It really is as simple as that.

If you can provide your child with **1) sufficient exposure to the target language(s); and 2) create a genuine need for your child to speak that language**, provided that your child has no developmental issues or learning difficulties, there is absolutely no reason why they won't become fluent in your chosen target language(s). But *both* conditions have to be met. You can't just have one without the other!

Human beings – children and grown-ups alike – require a vast amount of linguistic input in order to acquire a language, whether it's their mother tongue or additional languages. You must have heard the expression "children are like sponges!" many, many times. So surely that means I can just speak to my child in the target language every now and then, or perhaps introduce a little phrase here and there, and in time, they'll just "soak it all up", right?

Wrong!

I'm sorry, but this is just wishful thinking. The truth is, even sponges need to be fed. *A lot.* **Your child needs a huge amount of exposure to the target language in order to produce output**.

The next obvious question is: what constitutes "sufficient" exposure? Is it 5 hours a week? 10 hours a week? 30 hours a week? There is in fact no consensus among experts when it comes to this pretty basic question. **You may have heard of the "30% rule" – basically, the idea is that a child needs to be exposed to a language roughly 30% of their waking time in order to become fluent in that language.** Let's say a typical child is awake for 12 hours a day. 30% of those 12 hours would therefore translate into **3.6 hours a day, or 25.2 hours per week**.

Of course, the "30% rule" will not be true for everyone – people's individual abilities and circumstances are just far too variable for one rule to be applicable to all. However I think it's still a useful figure to bear in mind when planning how much exposure you need to work into your child's routine, or monitoring how much exposure they are getting.

And now it's time to define the term "exposure" too. **Not all kinds of "exposure" are equa**l – watching an hour of cartoons in the target language is *not* the same as one hour of reading stories and chatting about their day with mummy or daddy. Children need lots of *interaction* in order to acquire a language. **In short, your child needs high-quality exposure to the target language, and *lots* of it**.

Another thing to bear in mind is that **you should aim to broaden your child's sources of language exposure**. In practical terms, this means trying to give your child the opportunity to use the target language with people other than mummy and daddy, in as many different settings as possible. Why is this important? Your child becomes fluent in the majority language (e.g. English) through interacting with a countless number of people on a daily basis, all of whom have their own quirks when it comes to their pronunciation, word choices, sentence patterns and so on. From this rich and varied input, your child acquires the majority language in the most natural way and is capable of understanding a wide variety of speech in that language. You want to replicate this process as closely as possible in the target language.

So in real life, how do you go about replicating this process? **Try to make friends with other families in your area who speak your language. Explore weekend language school options. Enlist your parents' help,** if you're lucky enough to have them close by. Ideally you want your child to really understand that mummy/ daddy is not the only one who speaks this language; that lots of other people use it too in lots of different situations.

Having said that, varied exposure is optional rather than essential. It's perfectly possible for a child to acquire a language from one source alone, i.e. their parent(s). So if for whatever reason, you find yourself and/or your partner to be the only source(s) of input in the target language for your child, that's absolutely fine. In that case, focus on ensuring adequate high-quality exposure to the target language for your child.

But let's say your child *is* getting a good 30 hours of high-quality exposure to the language on a weekly basis. How come they're still not speaking the language?

This was exactly the problem I ran into with Alexey. I worked part-time as a freelancer and Alexey only went to nursery two/three afternoons a week. For at least eight hours a day, I was with him and speaking predominantly in Mandarin to him. So, why would he only talk to me in English?

Looking back on it now, I can clearly see that what was lacking was not exposure, but the *need* to speak the target language. When he talked to me in English, I did respond to him mostly in Mandarin but from his point of view, it was clear that 1) *mummy understands everything I say*; 2) *mummy would still cater to my needs when I speak to her English*. So why on earth would he speak to me in Mandarin, which at the time would have required so much more effort on his part?

There was literally zero need for him to do it. So why would he do it? It's only with the benefit of hindsight that I now see so clearly the issues that baffled me so much back then.

So, if your child is, for whatever reason, not able or willing to speak the target language, take a good hard look at these two things: exposure and need. Have both of these conditions been met? If not, what can you do about it? In the following chapters, I'll share with you lots of tips and advice to help you create and maintain these two conditions.

2. The sooner you start, the better (although it's never too late)

What's the best age to start introducing a second language? The answer is simple. **The earlier the better!** Most experts agree that the very earliest stages of language acquisition occur before a child is even born – around week 25 or 26 of pregnancy, babies in the womb have been shown to respond to voices and noise[ix]. One study clearly demonstrated that, in the later stages of pregnancy, unborn babies could not only differentiate their mother's voice from other people's voices; they could also distinguish their native language from a foreign language[x]. So babies begin to make sense of language and make their first baby-steps towards speech and socialisation before they're even born. By six months of age, infants already display preferences for phonemes (a unit of sound that can distinguish one word from another in a particular language) in their native language over those in foreign languages, and by the end of their first year no longer respond to phonetic elements peculiar to non-native languages[xi].

This is all great news if you're still planning your language strategy for an unborn child or a newborn. But what if your child is already slightly older, say two years old? Is your quest already doomed?

Do *not* despair! Even though the mantra of "The sooner you start, the better" is generally true, fortunately young children are extremely good at acquiring new skills, and this certainly includes learning languages. Opinions vary among experts, but **it is generally thought that up to the age of 10, children can acquire a new language and achieve native-like fluency and pronunciation**[xii]. So please don't assume that your child is too old. I know plenty of people who started learning a new language as adults and became genuinely fluent, with minimal "foreign" accent. So, no, your four-year-old is *really* not too old. See Chapter 7 for more tips and advice on how to help your slightly older child learn a new language.

3. Consistency, consistency, consistency

You may already have a family strategy of your own for raising your child with two or more languages (if not, please see Chapter 4 for an overview of the "Big Three" Strategies and Chapter 5 for formulating a strategy for your family). **No matter what your chosen strategy is, *stick to it*. Be consistent**. If you and your partner have decided to use the "One Parent, One Language" strategy, then make sure that you exclusively use your language with your child, and that your partner does the same. *All the time.* Or more realistically, aim for 95% of the time (I'll explain throughout this book why you may need to use the majority language 5% of the time). This is especially important when your child is not already fluent, and you're trying to establish the target language. Once the target language is well established – meaning that your child is fluent and is consistently using it with you – then some of these rules can be relaxed a little to allow for things like helping your child with homework in the majority language. But until you reach that stage, **it's important to be very disciplined about using the target language consistently**.

Why is consistency so important? Again, it goes back to Principle Number One: Exposure and Need. If you're only speaking the target language *some* of the time, not only are you effectively reducing your child's exposure to the language, but you are also sending out a message to your child that "mummy/ daddy speaks English (or whatever your majority language is) to me" which inevitably diminishes the need to use the target language from the child's perspective. Children (and humans in general) are smart and… lazy. All things being equal, we'll always choose the effort-saving option. If you present an easy option (i.e. speaking English) and a difficult option (i.e. speaking the target language which at this stage still feels like a chore) to your child, which one do you think they'll choose? **So until it becomes *effortless* for your child to speak the target language, it's best to err on the side of caution and avoid using the majority language as much as possible.**

4. Match your effort and commitment level to your desired goal

One basic question we haven't addressed so far is the definition of "bilingual" or "multilingual". For the sake of simplicity, let's focus on "bilingual" for now. What does it mean to be "bilingual"? To some people, it means being able to speak two languages fluently, with native-like pronunciation. To others, it means being able to communicate in these languages in everyday situations. Do you have to be able to read and write like a native speaker of your second language to consider yourself "bilingual"?

Everyone would have different answers to these questions, just as every parent would have different expectations of their child and desired goals. Some parents want their child to be equally fluent and literate in both the majority language and the target language(s). Some parents are happy for their child to have a passive knowledge of the target language but not necessarily be able to speak it. Some (like my husband and I) would like their child to be fluent enough to communicate in the target language, and later to acquire at the minimum basic literacy skills. The truth is, all these goals are equally valid and only you and your partner can decide on what's necessary for your family's needs.

But here comes the tricky bit – does your effort and commitment level match your desired goal? For example, let's say on a scale of 1 to 10, you and your partner would like your child to achieve a 9 in terms of fluency and literacy in the target language – you want them to be able to speak the target language fluently, without an accent, like a native speaker, and to have literacy skills comparable to a child of the same age who's a native speaker of the target language. This is an admirable and very ambitious goal. But you find that your child is perhaps "only" a 6 or 7 on that scale at this moment in time. They can communicate well in the target language in most situations but perhaps have a noticeable accent, or they struggle to string together more complicated sentences. They only have basic literacy skills, nowhere near comparable to a child of the same age "back home". You feel somewhat frustrated at your child's lack of progress. Chances are, the problem lies not with your child but with you (and/ or your partner): evaluate your effort and commitment level very honestly. On a scale of 1 to 10, are you operating at level 7 or 9? Are you spending enough time on literacy homework with your child? Is your child exposed to enough sophisticated language to help them express themselves more fluently and eloquently in the target language? **If you find that there's a mismatch between your desired goal and the effort + commitment level, you need to perform some sort of reassessment – either lower your goal, or up your effort. This way your expectations will be more realistic and you'll appreciate rather than feel disappointed by your child's achievements.**

5. Establish useful routines and stick to them

Children thrive on routine.

This applies to both language acquisition and general development. In one study, researchers examined the number of daily routines that more than 8,500 children practised with their families. They found that each "ritual" – such as having family dinner together, or participating in singing and reading together – was linked to a 47% increase in the odds that children would have strong emotional and social skills[xiii].

When it comes to language acquisition, in addition to using the target language consistently (see Principle Number Three above), I really recommend that you try to incorporate a few language-related routines into the family's daily life. **It's important that each routine is not too time-consuming that it feels onerous for both the child and parents; it should be something that can be easily slotted into the family's schedule and can realistically be maintained on most days. Think short-and-sweet: a 15-minute "study" session before or after dinner, plus 15 minutes of reading at bedtime would be a great start.** It's much better to stick to these 15-minute routines *every day* (or at least on most days), than cram in hours of work on the odd weekend here and there.

But what do you do if you have a really, *really* busy day, and you literally cannot even fit in a 15-minute session? In that case, I strongly suggest that you do a 5-minute session, or even a 3-minute session, rather than skip it entirely. The reason is that **every time you skip a session, it becomes easier to skip another one, and another one** (anyone who has experience of trying to go to the gym every day would be familiar with this scenario!) It's okay to have set days off, for example every Sunday, or even longer breaks during holidays. **But really adhering to a routine *every day* gives you the best chance of persevering, and helps your child understand what to expect**.

You may well find that your child cannot focus for 15 minutes and that's totally normal. Children have notoriously short attention spans – **a really useful rule of thumb I've come across during my research is to multiply your child's age by two, and that's the number of minutes your child is able to concentrate for**. For example, for a three-year-old child: 3 x 2 = 6 (minutes). If your child's attention span is significantly longer than what this formula indicates, that's fantastic. But if not, try to adjust your routine to your child's current attention span to minimise frustration on both sides.

To maximise your chance of success, **try to do the same activity at the same time every day**. This way it becomes automatic – everyone knows what to expect and the routine becomes firmly embedded into the family's daily life. In our household, my husband had been doing Russian homework with our children for 15-20 minutes after dinner almost every day for about one year, until recently – more on why later. And after each session, both children were then rewarded with a small treat to keep their motivation levels up. And the result has been amazing – this routine has really helped them grow their vocabulary and boosted their basic literacy skills. I started implementing a similar routine a few months ago to teach the kids some basic Chinese characters and the results have far exceeded my expectations. After a month, Alexey could already recognise about 100 characters and could even read some basic short sentences, and despite the occasional setbacks, he's making solid progress every day. Such is the power of routine!

However, it's important to be flexible too. Recently my husband noticed that the children sometimes had difficulty concentrating in the evening after a long day. He therefore made the decision to get up earlier in the morning (which is a *huge* sacrifice for a night-owl like my husband!) and do Russian homework with the kids after breakfast instead. The differences were very tangible. They children were generally in a better mood and were able to concentrate much better. The downside, however, was that the morning Russian homework routine seemed to deplete their energy and ability to concentrate for the Mandarin homework routine. This is completely normal as doing high-concentration activities requires lots of brainpower and literally depletes your blood glucose supply[xiv]. So I had to give them at least 10 minutes' break (and a quick snack to replenish those blood sugar levels!) before starting our Mandarin homework routine.

I'm fully aware that this is only possible because our children are not in full-time education yet, nor am I in full-time work. For most families, doing language homework in the morning before the school run may not be feasible. But remember, **you don't need to carve out a big chunk of time. 15 minutes of language homework after school, once the kids have had a snack and some rest, would be an excellent start.** Even for us, we'll have to tweak our schedule again when both children are in school full-time later this year but I have the confidence that we'll find a new schedule that works for us. And I have the confidence that you can, too.

Even if you do everything right, you *will* have good days and bad days. Like us, you'll probably find that your child is more motivated and focused on some days more than others, and that's totally normal. Don't feel discouraged! Just keep going and trust me, **you'll be amazed by how much you can achieve with short but consistent daily routines.**

6. You reap what you sow: why every little bit counts

The principle that you reap what you sow, or in other words, "you get what you put in", is one of those maxims that hold true in all aspects of life. When it comes to your child's language learning journey, you'll inevitably encounter lots of bumps along the way, and there will be days when the tedium of reading yet another book or slogging through yet another worksheet will really get to you, and you might find yourself wondering, "what's the point?" But always remember this: every little thing you do with your child today – that extra story you read together, that extra lullaby you sing at bedtime – will help your child flourish on their multilingual journey. Always bear in mind that your child's fluency in the target language will essentially be the sum total of everything they've done related to that language on a daily basis. There *is* no shortcut. There are no magic pill or brain implants (yet). And unless you "outsource" this process to a fully bilingual school, or a professional caregiver/ educator, *you* will be the one who's responsible for making the effort yourself and for creating the conditions for your child to make that effort!

Let me give you an example to illustrate the power of taking small steps every day: the Chinese writing system is notoriously difficult to get to grips with because there's no alphabet; all Chinese children have to learn thousands of characters by rote from a young age. In reality, however, a Chinese person only needs to know 1,500 to 2,000 characters to be *legally* recognised as literate, based on China's official national literacy policy. Those 1,500 to 2,000 characters represent a basic education level that can help you make it in day-to-day life[xv]. The trouble is, even 1,500 characters sounds like a heck of a lot to memorise!

But let's say you establish a 15-minute homework routine with your child starting from the age of five, teaching them the basics of Chinese reading and writing. I picked age five because it's more or less a happy medium – in China, children are introduced to reading and writing no later than age three, whereas in Europe many children are not taught reading and writing until age six or above. So OK, age five is a pretty uncontroversial age to start. And your goal is to teach your child *three* new characters a day.

I hope you'd agree that three new characters a day is a fairly realistic and modest goal. Even with my sluggish thirty-five-year-old brain, I *could* memorise three new words a day if I put my mind to it! But when you multiply that by 300 days (see how generous I am here, allowing you 65 days off a year!), it already amounts to 900 characters. If you simply continue at that pace, your child will know 1,800 characters by the age of *seven*.

According to the BBC's "Mini Guide" to the Chinese language[xvi], you need to know about 2,000 to 3,000 characters to be able to read a newspaper in Chinese. So by our calculation, your child can reach this goal by about age nine. A college-educated Chinese person knows about 8,000 characters, which sounds like an intimidatingly high figure. But if you stick to the three-character-a-day, 300-day-a-year routine, you can go from zero to 8,000 characters in 8.8 years, which means that by age fourteen, your child will know as many characters as an average college-educated Chinese person. Obviously I'm massively oversimplifying here – most Chinese words are made up of more than one character and simply knowing 8,000 individual characters doesn't necessarily mean you can make sense of a newspaper article in real life, but I hope I've convinced you of the importance of the little steps you take every day. This is truly a wonder on a par with the magic of compound interest!

So in one word – persevere. And persevere some more.

7. Focus on what your child *can* do, not what your child *can't* do

Believe me: this small but significant adjustment in your mindset and perception will make a *huge* difference. Let me begin by admitting that I myself have at times been terribly guilty of focusing on what my child *can't* do – more than once, I have shouted at my son in frustration because he can't remember a certain Chinese character that we've reviewed for what feels like a hundred times. What's worse – and this is a terrible confession for any parent to make – I have even called him "stupid" in moments of extreme frustration once or twice – something I swore I would *never* do, and it always made me feel terrible and tearful with guilt afterwards.

You may have experienced a similar feeling of annoyance and frustration with your own child, which is totally understandable. As "wise", knowledgeable grown-ups, it's sometimes difficult for us to understand why it's just *so damn hard* for a child to say something correctly, or even just to remember a word that they've seen or heard a million times!

But every time you catch yourself thinking like this, please pause for a moment and perform a little mental switch: **instead of focusing on what your child can*not* do, really try to remind yourself how much they *can* do, and how much they *have* achieved.** For me, I have to constantly remind myself that, No, my son is not somehow "stupid" because he can't recite *The Three Hundred Tang Poems* by heart, a feat that apparently every preschooler in China seems capable of. He is not "stupid" for not conjugating his Russian verbs correctly every time, as many of his friends from Russian school are able to do.

I now tell myself that, as a matter of fact, it is *amazing* that he can speak three languages, however imperfectly, at the age of four. It is *amazing* that he now knows over a hundred Chinese characters, and can even read short sentences in a language that he only speaks at home. **This is not about being boastful** – you don't have to shout from the rooftop "MY CHILD CAN SPEAK THREE/ FOUR/ FIVE LANGUAGES!!!"; **this is about being rightfully proud of your child's achievements, however modest they may seem.** When you adjust your mindset like this, you would come to appreciate your child's achievements, rather than feel annoyed, frustrated or worse, ashamed. Once you've flipped this mental switch, you would feel so much more positive, and this positivity would inevitably rub off on your child, creating a virtuous circle.

So please do your best to resist the temptation to compare your child or your family to others. At risk of sounding clichéd, the only yardstick against which you should compare your child is, well, your child himself/ herself!

In the next chapter, I will take you through the "Big Three Strategies" most commonly adopted by bilingual and multilingual families, with plenty of examples to show you how they work in practice.

CHAPTER 4

THE "BIG THREE" STRATEGIES

In this chapter, I will give you a quick overview of the "Big Three Strategies" for raising bilingual and multilingual children, with plenty of examples to show you how these strategies work in real life, and how to overcome potential pitfalls. As with the rest of this book, I'll focus on the practical, as opposed to the theoretical aspects.

Whatever stage you're at – whether you're still planning your language strategy in preparation for the birth of your first child, or you're already engaged in daily language battles with a strong-willed pre-schooler – I hope you'll find something useful in this section.

Needless to say, real life can be messy. It often defies categorisation, and you may well find that you'll be using a mix of strategies, which is absolutely fine – there are truly as many language strategies as there are families. Your family is unique. Your child is unique. Your personal philosophy is unique. Your family's circumstances are unique. So why shouldn't your family's language strategy be? Take on board what's useful for your child and family, make it your own, and enjoy the journey!

1. One Parent, One Language (OPOL)

What it says on the tin! In a two-parent household, one parent would always speak one language with the child, while the other parent would always speak the other language.

OPOL for BILINGUAL families

If you are hoping to raise your child to be BILINGUAL (i.e. the majority language of your place of residence + a minority language, which is also the target language for your child), your set-up might look something like this:

Example:

Emily and Diego live in the UK. Emily was born and raised in England and has only limited knowledge of Spanish. Diego is from Mexico and while his mother tongue is Spanish, he is also fluent in English. They communicate with each other in English. They want to raise their daughter Mariana to be *bilingual* in English and Spanish. In this case, Emily would speak to Mariana only in English, and Diego would use Spanish exclusively.

Potential problems:

One parent speaks English and one parent speaks Spanish… Classic OPOL – so far so good! But what about when *all three of them are together*? Or when the parents are talking among themselves, in the child's presence?

Strict proponents of OPOL would advise that, when all three of them are conversing together, each parent should stick to their respective languages when directly addressing the child, but can switch to English – their only mutual language – when they are addressing each other. Adam Beck, the author of *Maximize Your Child's Bilingual Ability*, who raised his children to be bilingual in Japanese and English, takes a *really* strict approach: he and his wife avoid having lengthy conversations in Japanese (their mutual language and the majority language of their country of residence) in the children's presence; what's more, he even actively avoided social gatherings that would require him to speak Japanese extensively in the children's presence. The purpose of this rather "extreme" approach, he explains, is to reinforce the message that "Daddy only speaks English", and therefore the *need* to use that language exclusively with Daddy. But even the author himself admits that his own approach is unusual in its strictness.

A similarly strict approach could work for you, of course, but in reality you might decide to do what feels the most natural for your family. You might find it more natural for all three of you to converse in English together, for example. As long as this does not impact on your child's ability to speak the target language, it shouldn't be a problem.

With my own kids, I speak to them in Chinese 95% of the time when I'm directly addressing them, even when there are non-Chinese speakers present, but we do live in an area where bilingualism is very common and doing this would not cause awkwardness. However, if a conversation *directly* involves other non-Chinese speakers, I do switch to English to be polite. For example, a mum at the playground offers Alexey a biscuit, with me next to him. In this situation, I would ask him in English if he wants a biscuit, and remind him to say "thank you" in English. The funny thing is, even if I address him in English in this sort of situation now, 90% of the time he would reply to me in Chinese!

OPOL for TRILINGUAL families

If you're hoping to raise your child to be TRILINGUAL (i.e. the majority language of your place of residence + one target language from one parent + another target language from the other parent), OPOL might be your best starting point; you might find yourself and your partner practising OPOL without even being aware of it! Since this is essentially what my husband and I do with our kids, I'll use our family as a real-life example.

Example:

I speak Mandarin and my husband Kirill speaks Russian. We live in the UK, where English is the majority language. Both children were born in the UK and live in an environment where English is the majority language in all settings. I use Mandarin exclusively with the children, and Kirill only uses Russian with them. At home, when all four of us are together, I try to speak Russian as much as possible but in reality I use a mix of English and Russian.

Potential problems:

The OPOL is the language strategy of choice for many, if not most trilingual families as the numbers just add up rather nicely. Each parent would use one language exclusively, and the child will acquire the majority language from the wider community. But as with bilingual families, the question as to which language should be used when all the family members are together can be a tricky one. In our family, since my husband doesn't speak any Chinese, whereas I know some basic Russian, we have settled on Russian as the "family language" when all of us are together but in reality, I have no choice but to switch to English sometimes as I simply don't know how to say more complicated things in Russian. It may not be ideal but in our particular case, we feel that this set-up, albeit imperfect, helps bolster Russian for the kids as they get less exposure to it throughout the day.

If you and your partner *do* speak each other's languages, you may well find that when the whole family's together, a mix of languages is used and that's okay – a natural pattern will eventually emerge and as long as you continue to use OPOL consistently with your child when alone with them, it will still work.

If you and your partner do not speak each other's languages, then obviously when the whole family is together, you and your partner will converse in your common language (e.g. English); but what about your child? In this scenario, would the parents make a concession and use the majority language (assuming it's the same as your common language) with the child? Would it cause confusion?

Unfortunately, there are no straightforward answers to such questions. I wish there were too! Each family and each child is different and you'll have to find your family's happy equilibrium. Experiment and see what works best for your family's unique circumstances. **You may find that when the whole family is together, it feels more natural to just use the majority language together so everyone can enjoy naturally flowing conversation. As long as your child's fluency in the two target languages does not suffer, you can just continue to use the majority language as the shared family language. However, if you see signs that your child is not getting enough exposure to the target languages, or your child begins to address you in the majority language more frequently, you will have to adjust your strategy and try to minimise the use of English even when the whole family's together.**

The bottom line is that there are no hard and fast rules when it comes to the implementation of the OPOL strategy, or indeed any language strategy. **Bringing up bilingual/ multilingual children is *not* an exact science**, which can be frustrating for some but also gives you the freedom to experiment and find out what's right for your family!

The second potential problem for trilingual families who adopt the OPOL strategy is that it's often difficult to ensure that the child gets adequate exposure to each of the target languages, especially if one or both parents work full-time.

In this case, the parents should aim to:

✓**Make the most of the evening with the child.** For two parents in full-time work, this probably equates to two to three hours per day, split between two target languages, which is not a lot. If possible, switch off the TV and make sure you spend lots of quality time together, talking a lot! **Talk about your day at the dinner table together. Get the kids involved in any necessary household chores** – this is a great way for them to acquire the target language in a fun, natural way and, well, since you would spend that chunk of time on those chores anyway, why not factor in just a little extra time (because getting little kiddies to "help" will inevitably mean taking more time to finish a task, not less) and turn it into a language-learning activity? Win-win!

Bath-time and bedtime are also the perfect opportunities for some parent-child bonding, as well as fun language learning! **Aim for 15 minutes of reading before bed in your target languages** – this should be one routine to stick to, no matter what.

If you and your partner struggle to find the time to interact intensively with your child due to work or other commitments, consider hiring an after-school nanny, au pair or babysitter who speaks the target language(s). Ideally you should have one hired person for each of your target languages, of course, to ensure even exposure to both target languages. But in reality, this might be quite difficult to arrange! You may find that local nannies in one of your target languages are not easy to come by; you may, as a family, decide that one of the target languages should take priority for your family's needs at this moment in time. In any case, **if the child is not exposed to both target languages equally during the week, make sure that you really focus on making up for the "neglected" language on weekends.**

Other families – where one parent spends significantly more time with the child than the other – might face different challenges. In our household, my husband works full-time while I, as a freelancer, spend a lot more time with the children, both of whom go to nursery part-time only. As a result, their Chinese has always been considerably stronger than their Russian. As mentioned previously, to compensate for this, my husband and I agreed that I should try to speak Russian as much as possible when we are with the kids. To be totally honest, since I only speak really basic Russian, this is not always practical but on the whole it's a workable strategy for us and really gives me the extra motivation to improve my Russian. Your family set-up will be different from mine but I'm certain that you and your partner can find your own way of balancing the two target languages. **If you'd like to have a more precise picture of your child's language environment, you can try tracking your child's exposure to all their languages (majority language + target language(s)) over the course of one week and see if there are any obvious imbalances. A simple Excel spreadsheet will do the job!**

To conclude, if you decide that OPOL is broadly speaking the best strategy for your family, don't be afraid to modify it to suit your family's needs.

2. Minority Language at Home (ML@H)

This approach mostly applies to BILINGUAL families. Typically, both parents speak the same minority language, and the family lives in a country/region where a different language – the majority language – is spoken. So essentially, the child gets the minority language from their parents, and the majority language from the wider community. As the child "only" has to juggle two languages, and both parents speak the same minority language at home, it should be easier to achieve the 30% exposure (as discussed previously, this is just a ballpark figure) needed for effective language acquisition.

Statistically speaking, ML@H is a very effective strategy for raising bilingual children. According to one study, up to 93% of families who practise ML@H succeed in passing on the minority language to their children[xvii]. From my own observations, when both parents speak the same language at home and they use it more or less exclusively with their children, in most cases the children do end up bilingual fairly effortlessly. One caveat: this only applies to listening and speaking of course. Reading and writing is a whole different ball game!

If neither of you are a native speaker of the minority/ target language, or maybe only one of you is a native speaker, ML@H can still work.

It would be an excellent opportunity for the non-native speaker to improve their language skills! And do not be afraid to make mistakes. Your partner (if you're the non-native speaker) can correct you and in time, your child will help you improve too!

Potential problems:

What if you find yourself among the 7% of families who fail to pass on the minority language to their children? This can be down to a number of factors:

- The parents (or at least one parent) are not using the minority language consistently enough. (See Chapter 1: The Seven Key Principles: Principle Number Three) Remember, always aim to use the target language with your child at least 95% of the time. That's a somewhat arbitrary figure but basically, you should be using the target language almost exclusively and that 5% is only there to make allowance for inevitable things like talking to other families in the playground or completing homework that requires using the majority language etc. Be really mindful about how often you use the majority language – I know how easy it is to slip into the majority language when it's literally all around you, but if you want to maximise your child's chance of success, you simply have to minimise your use of the majority language. It's as simple as that. However, if your child is already fluent, you can be more relaxed about using the majority language.

✓Action point: Start monitoring your use of the majority language today. Aim for 95% exclusivity in terms of using the target language/ home language.

- The child is able to speak the home language at first, but gradually loses it once they start full-time nursery/ school. To avoid this problem, some experts suggest delaying your child's introduction to the majority language for as long as possible; in reality this means not sending them to a full-time majority-language nursery/ school until the home language is fully established. Or even better, send them to a bilingual nursery/ school. For many parents though, this is simply not an option. These days, a large proportion of families rely on two incomes and have no choice but to send their children to nursery full-time when they turn one or even earlier. In some cases, the majority language just "takes over" as the child spends more and more time away from home.

If this is happening to your child, first of all, be assured that it's totally normal. You should be celebrating the fact that they are learning a new language and are interacting with their peers. However, it's really important to reinforce the home language as soon as you see signs of what I call "majority- language invasion". If your child starts using English words at home, you need to gently but firmly reassert the home language. Every time they say an English word or phrase, ask them to say it again in the home language, or at the very least repeat it in the home language yourself so they can hear the "correct" language input. However, if the "invasion" is at a more advanced stage, meaning that your child is no longer able or willing to speak the home language, you may want to consider implementing "The Bootcamp Method" (see Chapter 6 for details) as soon as possible before the majority language takes over completely!

✓Action point: Delay your child's introduction to the majority language for as long as possible. If that's not an option, make sure you're very strict about using the minority language when they're with you, and implement "The Bootcamp Method" (Chapter 6) if necessary.

3. Time and Place (T&P)

Using the Time and Place strategy, the parents would separate the languages used with the child either by time or by place (or both), which means that in theory, there's no upper limit to the number of languages used. In reality, however, most parents would limit it to a maximum of four or five languages.

T&P is particularly useful if the parents: 1) want their child to be fluent in four or more languages; or 2) want to gradually introduce a second/ third/ fourth language. It can also be adopted in combination with OPOL and ML@H.

So how does this strategy work in more concrete terms? For the first scenario (**i.e. Parents who want their child to be fluent in four or more languages**), let's take a look at the following example.

Example:

Marion is from France; her mother tongue is French but she's also fluent in Spanish and English as a result of her family background and professional experience. Her partner Andrea is from Germany; his mother tongue is German but due to his work and education, he's also fluent in English and Spanish, in addition to some basic knowledge of French. The couple lives in New York City with their son Luc (aged four), who attends a bilingual German and English pre-school. At home, Andrea speaks German to Luc, and Marion speaks French to him. When all three are together, they speak in French as much as possible even though Andrea is not fluent. This decision is motivated by the need to bolster French, as Luc already gets plenty of exposure to German at pre-school.

The family also has a Mexican nanny who looks after Luc for approximately 15 hours a week. She speaks to Luc exclusively in Spanish. As both Andrea and Marion are fluent in Spanish, they decided to use Spanish with Luc every Saturday in order to reinforce his Spanish.

By separating the languages by time and place, Marion and Andrea enable Luc to gain a good amount of exposure to all four languages:

English (the majority language of New York City, U.S.), French (Mum's language and the family's "home language"), German (Dad's language and one of the languages used at pre-school) as well as Spanish (Nanny's language and the family's "Saturday" language).

For the second scenario (i.e. **Parents who want to gradually introduce a third/ fourth language**), let's look at another hypothetical example.

Example:

Oksana and Viktor are from Ukraine; they're both fluent in Ukrainian, Russian and English. The family lives in London, UK. They have been using ML@H with their daughter Anna from birth, speaking to her exclusively in Ukrainian. By the age of two, Anna can understand and speak Ukrainian and English at an age-appropriate level. At this point, the parents decide to introduce a third language – Russian. Their goal is for Anna to become trilingual in Ukrainian, Russian and English.

Oksana starts speaking to Anna in Russian at lunchtime only, in order to introduce a new language gradually. Once Anna is more comfortable with this, Oksana encourages her to speak Russian at lunchtime.

After a month, Oksana starts speaking to Anna in Russian when they are out and about. There are many Russian-speaking families in their area and it's easy to find other Russian-speaking children to play with in their local parks and playgrounds. Ultimately, Oksana and Viktor want to make Ukrainian the home language, and Russian the language of the "outside world", alongside English.

In this case, the family's language strategy may evolve into some form of OPOL – maybe Viktor will primarily use Ukrainian with Anna, and Oksana Russian. **T&P is flexible enough to accommodate for customisation and change of circumstances.**

51

Having said that, for T&P to work well, consistency *is* important. Once you've decided which language to use in which time and place, try your best to stick to it, at least until a change of circumstances demands an adjustment in your strategy.

Now that we've had a look at the "Big Three Strategies", I will take you through the process of formulating a unique strategy for your family step-by-step in the next chapter.

CHAPTER 5

FORMULATING A STRATEGY FOR YOUR FAMILY

Now that we've had a look at the Big Three strategies, it's time to formulate a unique plan for your family that's tailor-made for your needs and circumstances. In this chapter, I will take you through this potentially daunting process step-by-step. On my website (www.multilingualfamilyhub.com), you can download a free Family Language Plan template to get you started!

Step 1: Define your goals

As with any other goal in life, to achieve a goal, you first need to *define* it. **Which languages do you want your child to speak, and at what fluency level?** There's a common preconception that being bilingual/ multilingual means being *fully* and *equally* fluent in two or more languages. In reality, no one acquires two or more languages in the exact same circumstances, and similarly, no one *uses* two or more languages in the exact same circumstances or for the same purposes. The "perfection" preconception puts too much pressure on parents who wish to raise bilingual or multilingual children, as many feel that they have only succeeded if their child is equally fluent in *all* their languages.

As mentioned in Chapter 3, under Principle Number Four, all parents have different goals in terms of the level of fluency they'd like their child to achieve, and these goals can roughly be graded on a scale of 1 to 10. This rather crude grading system is only a tool to help you align your effort and commitment level to your goal; in reality all goals are valid, and only you can decide what these goals are. And of course, these goals can evolve and shift, depending on your family's circumstances and your child's development. You can do your best to guide and nurture your child but at the end of the day, you don't have total control over the outcome – this applies as much to their linguistic development as to every other aspect of your child's life. Remember – they are individual human beings just like us grown-ups. There is a (very small) possibility that despite all your effort, your child will not want to speak more than one language. That doesn't mean you've failed as a parent.

Nevertheless, in the planning stages, it's useful to have some concrete goals in place, even if you'll have to revise them perhaps many times as you go along. Remember that language learning is always an ongoing journey – every day we live on this earth, we are learning and evolving. Your child's language goals will keep evolving too. Be prepared to be flexible and adapt your strategy as you go along.

Step 2: Pick a strategy, or mix-and-match

Which one of the "Big Three" strategies is the most appropriate or practical for your family's circumstances? Remember, you don't have to adhere to a single strategy religiously – in the early stages, it's often a good idea to choose one strategy just to give yourself a starting point, and to have some basic principles to guide you. Quite often, one of the three strategies will jump out at you as the most obvious candidate: for example, let's say both you and your partner are from France and are starting a family in London, the Minority Language at Home (ML@H) strategy would be the natural choice; or if you're originally from Japan, and your partner from Poland, and you are starting a family in the U.S., you may find that you naturally gravitate towards the One Parent One Language (OPOL) strategy. If your family's circumstances are slightly more complicated, or perhaps you and/or your partner are fluent in multiple languages, you may well decide to start with the Time & Place (T&P) strategy, or alternatively, you may choose to start with OPOL first, and introduce further languages with T&P further down the line, depending on your child's progress and your family's circumstances.

This process is not unlike the process of outlining a novel – you sketch out a blueprint at the beginning just to give yourself a sense of direction and structure, but during the actual writing process, characters can take on a life of their own, and plot lines can take a surprising turn that you didn't foresee. The point is that the outline is not set in stone. It should and will adapt to the flow of your story. So should your language strategy.

Step 3: Figure out *"who* does *what* and *when"*

Now that you have decided on one of the "Big Three" strategies, or devised a plan of your own, the next step is to figure out **"who does what and when"**. **To do so, it's crucial to decide upon the following: Which parent will speak which language (the "who"); which parent will be responsible for various activities (the "what"); and finally, when will each language be introduced?**

Let's look at an example. Imagine you're a native Spanish speaker, and your partner a native Korean speaker, and you both live in Australia. You and your partner have decided that your goal is to raise your child to be trilingual in Spanish, Korean and English, and that OPOL will be your family's chosen strategy. In this set-up, you will naturally speak Spanish to your child, and your partner Korean. English will come from the wider community. Since English is the only mutual language you and your partner share, you've both decided to continue to use English when conversing with each other, even in your child's presence. If the child is included in the conversation, you have the choice of using English or switching back to OPOL when directly addressing the child.

And when it comes to the "Who" component, don't forget to think beyond your immediate nuclear family. What role, if any, will grandparents play? If you have grandparents who speak the target language living nearby, this is absolutely one of the most valuable resources you should utilise. Explain your strategy to them and get them on board – they are likely to be very supportive of the idea of speaking their own language to their grandchild.

What role will your child's childcare and/or educational settings play? Will you consider sending your child to a fully bilingual nursery or school? Will you be using a nanny/ child-minder/ au pair who speaks the target language in order to maximise your child's exposure to the language? All of these factors should be given some consideration in the planning stage. See Chapter 7 for more tips on how to utilise these "human resources".

The "When" question can be addressed on two levels: on a broader level, you need to decide – or at least start thinking about – when would be the best time to introduce the target language. If you're trying to raise your child with three or more languages, then you need to think more specifically about when would be the best time to introduce each of the target languages. On a day-to-day level, you need to think about how each of the languages fits into your family's daily schedule, especially if you're practising some version of the Time and Place strategy.

Step 4: Find resources

In Step 3, I already covered some of the "human resources" aspects as they form part of the broader "Who does what and when" question. **Now that you have all the key players in place, it's time to start looking for material resources specific to your target language(s).**

The most important piece of kit in your language toolbox should be books. I'm not talking about language textbooks (although they can potentially play a role when your child is older) – what you need are lots of fun, colourful board books, picture books and story books in your target language(s). The Usborne "First Hundred Words" and "First Thousand Words" series are brilliant – if you don't have any suitable books yet, definitely consider making these the first books in your collection. We bought these in both the Chinese and Russian versions when Alexey was a baby, and four years on, we're still getting so much use out of them! They introduce lots of useful vocabulary with attractive, detail-rich illustrations based on scenes from everyday life. Once the kids are a bit older, these books will be an invaluable aid for building the foundation of literacy skills too.

Needless to say, the Internet and Amazon in particular are the easiest places to source books in your target language. **But you should also research specialist physical bookshops that stock children's books in your target language(s)** – these bookshops aren't always easy to find but can be such valuable resources. In London we found a couple of good Russian bookshops and a few Chinese bookshops where we could browse the books prior to purchasing them, and this is a great experience for children.

Some big chain bookshops also have dedicated foreign-language sections that are worth exploring. Waterstones in Piccadilly, for example, has a substantial section dedicated to Russian books, including children's books.

Libraries are also an invaluable resource. Many of them stock books in foreign languages; contact your local library to see what they have and you may be surprised! In the UK, many libraries will reserve and transfer specific books from other libraries within the same council for a small fee; in Hertfordshire, where we live now, this service is free for children's books.

While physical books are without a doubt the best option for very young children, slightly older children can also benefit from digital books, which can be easier to access. In Chapter 9, I've listed some resources to help you find digital books in your target language(s).

Once your child's a bit older, you may want to source some workbooks or worksheets with fun activities and more structured literacy activities. This is especially relevant if you decide to establish a homework routine (more on this in Chapter 7). Again, the Internet and Amazon could be your first port of call. On Amazon you should be able to find workbooks in most of the more widely-spoken foreign languages. If you manage to find bookshops that specialise in your target language(s), they are bound to stock such workbooks too. But you don't have to spend a fortune on buying workbooks. **The Internet is full of free resources – just Google "free printable worksheet in [your target language]" and you should be able to find a ton of free printable activities.**

In Chapter 8 and Chapter 9, you'll find a lot more activity ideas and tips on finding the right resources.

Step 5: Find support

The old adage that "It takes a whole village to raise a child" is just as applicable to raising a bilingual or multilingual kid – the wider your support network, the higher your child's chance of success will be. Oh, and the saner and happier *you* will be! Support comes in many shapes and forms. I've listed some of potential support networks below:

- **Other families**: if you live in a relatively large town or city, chances are you can find other families who speak your target language(s). Seek them out! Be proactive. If you're at the playground and you hear parents speaking to their kids in your target language, don't be afraid to strike up a conversation – most parents are more friendly and helpful than you might expect. Some of them may be just as eager as you are to meet other families who speak the same language. Perhaps you find the idea of striking up a conversation with strangers slightly intimidating? As one writer put it most succinctly, children are the best "social lubricant" you can have, even better than alcohol! Once you've become acquainted with particular families, why not arrange a play-date? Even if the children speak in English between themselves, it's still really beneficial for them to hear adults other than their own parents speaking the target languages. And you'll all appreciate talking to someone going through the same thing as yourselves, who can share your frustration and maybe pass on some useful tips too.

- **Your local children's centre**: Before the pandemic hit, my kids and I were regulars at our local Sure Start Children's Centre, which was like a second home to us. It's a great place to meet other families and to have a bit of adult conversation – very important especially if you're a part-time or full-time stay-at-home parent. Staff at children's centres can also give you free, friendly advice on your child's language development, or refer you to the relevant specialists. At our local children's centre a language specialist came to visit regularly and everyone could have an informal chat with them without an appointment. So as soon as your local children's centre re-opens, do check it out – you may make some new friends and meet other families who speak your target language(s) too.

- **Online communities for bilingual/ multilingual families**: Thanks to the Internet, it's never been easier to connect with other families who are trying to raise bilingual/ multilingual kids. If you live in an area where families who speak your target languages are far and few between, you should have no trouble finding families with your language combination on the World Wide Web. Apart from practical tips and advice, these online communities can also be a great source of moral support. In Chapter 9, you'll find a list of some useful websites where you can connect with other bilingual/ multilingual families.

- **Playgroups and classes**: At the time of writing, the pandemic has forced most playgroups and kids' classes to close temporarily; but once things return to normal, you should definitely try to find out if there are any playgroups and classes specific to your target languages in your local area. In the area where we used to live, there were numerous classes for young children such as French nursery rhyme sessions, many of which took place at our local library. So as soon as your local library opens, check out the posters on the bulletin boards or speak to the staff to find out more. You'll also find out about these activities from speaking to other parents. Alternatively, Google is always your best friend!

- **Language schools**: Depending on the popularity of your target languages, you may be able to find weekend schools specifically aimed at teaching children that language. In the UK, many of these weekend schools hire premises from local schools on the weekend. If you live in a large city, chances are a weekend school for your target language *does* exist – our Mongolian friend in London informed me that she'd found a weekend Mongolian language school in London, which is quite amazing considering the entire Mongolian population in the city number less than 1,000, according to the 2011 census! These schools can be a great way to boost your child's exposure to the target language, and to meet other families who speak the language. Our children's Russian school also sends us lots of worksheets and additional materials on a regular basis, which has been very useful in helping us establish and maintain a homework routine. So whether or not you wish to enrol your child at one of these schools, it's definitely worth investigating the options in your area. In Chapter 7, I've devoted an entire section to the subject of weekend language schools; so if this is something of interest to you, make sure you don't miss that section!

Step 6: Put everything into practice

Now that you've set out your goals, and have a strategy in place, or at least some sort of road map to guide you through the initial stages of your journey; you've figured out who's responsible for what and when; you've gathered some resources to get you started; you've hopefully established a bit of a support network – you are good to go! In fact, *don't* feel like you have to complete all of the above five steps before you can make a start. I'd say only steps 1 and 2 are absolutely essential at the beginning; the rest can be worked out or revisited as you go along.

No matter which strategy you've decided to adopt, always remember the Seven Key Principles, as set out in the previous chapter. Here's a quick recap of these seven principles:

1. The golden equation: BILINGUAL SUCCESS = EXPOSURE + NEED
2. The sooner you start, the better (although it's never too late)
3. Consistency, consistency, consistency
4. Match your effort and commitment level to your desired goal
5. Establish useful routines and stick to them
6. You reap what you sow – that's why every little bit counts!
7. Focus on what your child *can* do, not what your child *can't* do

So, if you haven't already started, begin talking to your child (or even unborn baby!) in the target language *today.* There is no better time to start. And there's one more mantra that I think is really relevant when it comes to raising a bilingual or multilingual child – and indeed when it comes to most things in parenting and life in general – ***Perfect is the enemy of good.*** I know there are many perfectionists among us, but if the desire for perfection is holding you back, it's time to break free from the tyrannical claws of perfectionism. As an analogy, think about how many people you know who've said that they want to write a novel, but because they only want to write the *perfect* novel, end up with *no novel* at all? Or the person who says he wants to learn Spanish but tells himself that there's no point because he'll never sound like a native speaker? And the truth is, when it comes to passing on a language to your child, the end result is not just up to you. Your child is the other (more important) half of this equation, and no matter what you'd like to think, you do not have control over your child's ability and aptitude. So forget about perfection. Nourish them, guide them, and hopefully they *will* thrive.

So, are you ready to map out a plan for your family? Don't forget to download a free Family Language Plan template from my website (www.multilingualfamilyhub.com)!

In the next chapter, I will tackle one of the most common issues faced by parents: what can you do when your child understands everything you say in the target language, but just will *not* speak it? Sounds like you and your child? Maybe it's time to give "The Bootcamp Method" a go! Read on to find out more…

CHAPTER 6

"MY CHILD ALWAYS REPLIES IN ENGLISH" HOW TO OVERCOME THE PASSIVE-TO-ACTIVE BARRIER WITH THE BOOTCAMP METHOD

In Chapter 1, I briefly touched on my struggle with getting my son to reply to me in Chinese, and how a chance encounter with another parent helped me overcome this problem, laying the foundation for what was later formulated into "The Bootcamp Method". In this chapter, I will take you through this method step-by-step.

The "My-child-always-replies-in-English" problem is surprisingly common. I've lost count of the number of parents who've told me about their struggle with this particular problem. Typically, the child understands the target language very well, as they get plenty of exposure to the language. In linguistic terms, this is referred to as the child's **"receptive language"**. When it comes to the acquisition of the majority language, a child normally progresses from acquiring "receptive language" to producing output (what linguists refer to as **"expressive language"**) naturally, without any special effort or intervention. However, when it comes to the acquisition of the minority language(s), some children struggle to make the transition from input to output. Why does this happen?

At the risk of sounding repetitive, it all boils down to the **exposure + need** equation, as per Principle One of the Seven Key Principles in Chapter 3. Put simply, if your child is getting sufficient exposure to the target language, and feels a genuine need to use the target language to have their needs met, they absolutely should be able to speak the target language. The Bootcamp Method mostly addresses the second part of the equation; it is in my opinion a highly effective way to create the need for your child to speak the target language.

But before we proceed, let's get a few things out of the way. **Firstly, I'm not saying that "something's wrong" if your child can understand the target language but is not able or willing to speak it.** The reason is twofold. Firstly, your child may simply be going through a developmental phase and that even without intervention, they will eventually start speaking the target language. This is especially relevant if your child is very young, say under three years old. Secondly, even if that transition doesn't happen, you and your partner may be genuinely content with the fact that your child has a good passive knowledge of the language, which can be built on in the future.

However, based on my experience with my own children, and observation of many other multilingual families, the "My-child-always-replies-in-English" problem seems to be very common, and is a problem that *does* cause frustration among a large number of parents who find themselves in this situation. Some of these parents have come to terms with this and are genuinely happy to carry on with the status quo; some are convinced that it's just a phase, and hope that their children will start speaking the language one day. And these are all valid decisions. As I said in Chapter 3, only you can decide what your goals are for your child, and it's okay to revise these goals along the way too.

If you're hoping that your child will make the "passive-to-active" switch on their own, I just want to point out that, **based on my observation, children who don't make this "switch" by the time they're three or four rarely make that switch later on, without intervention or a change in their linguistic environment**. At that age, most children start pre-school and that's when the influence of the majority language really becomes dominant. So if by this age, your child can understand but still doesn't speak your language, it's best not to assume that somehow they will start speaking it later on. Sadly, often the reverse is true – I've met quite a few parents who told me that their child was fluent in the minority language before they started pre-school, but then gradually lost it, as little or no effort was made to bolster the home language.

If like me, you're one of those parents who do want to take proactive action to help your child make that "switch", I really think that "The Bootcamp Method" could work for you, as it did for us. Here I just want to emphasise that this method is what personally worked for us, and that some experts actually advise against the "repetition" model, which forms the basis of "The Bootcamp Method". Experts in that camp recommend a more "gentle" approach, whereby the parent would simply continue to talk to the child in the target language, and if the child replies in their preferred language, the parent would simply repeat what was said by the child in the target language but not make the child repeat it. The technical term for this technique is "modelling" – the parent would "model" the correct speech in the target language.

If this gentle approach works for you, that's great! But chances are, you're *already* doing that and your child still hasn't made that "switch". So if this gentle approach doesn't work for you – and frankly, it didn't work for us – I urge you to give "The Bootcamp Method" a try. **I have full confidence that if you follow all the steps as outlined below, you too can help activate your child's bilingual ability, and help them make that passive-to-active switch!**

A step-by-step guide

- **Starting from now, make sure you speak to your child *exclusively* in your target language (aim for at least 95%).** At the beginning of this process it's really important to be strict and consistent. Once fluency is established, it's possible to relax this rule a little.

- **When your child talks to you in English** (or whatever the majority language/ the child's dominant language is), **make them repeat the same thing in the target language.**
- **Even if it's a full sentence, repeat it for the child until they can reproduce this utterance in its entirety; if need be, break the sentence down into smaller segments.** At first, the child is just parroting you, but through repetition, the vocabulary and grammatical structures will embed themselves in the child's brain. Each repetition is a form of consolidation.

Example: the basic "Bootcamp Method" technique

Child: "Mummy, I want some water." [The child says this in English]

Parent: *"Qing shuo, mama, wo xiang he shui."* [The parent says this in Mandarin, the target language. Translation: "Please say, 'mama, I want to have some water.'"]

(Child looks confused and angry!)

Child: "Mama, I want water!"

Parent: [Speaks very slowly and clearly] *"Qing shuo, mama, wo xiang he shui."*

Child: Hmmm… Uh… Mama, *wo…* I can't say it!

Parent: Wo xiang he shui.

Child: Wo… wo xiang he shui.

- **The key is consistency.** You should try to do this every time your child talks to you in his dominant/ preferred language. If you don't do it consistently, you will still see progress over a longer period of time, but progress will be much more gradual.

- **If you think your child is capable of saying this particular phrase or sentence in the target language, *prompt* them to say it.** If that word or phrase is already lodged somewhere in the child's brain, prompting them to retrieve that information and actively produce the desired output is more effective than just giving them the word or phrase "on a plate", so to speak. **Every time your child actively retrieves that information (even with the help of prompts), it's strengthening relevant neural connections in the brain. With time, it will become natural and automatic.**

Here's an example of a possible scenario, where prompting is used:

Example: how to use prompts

Child: Mama, I want some water.

Parent: *Ni hui yong Zhongwen shuo ma?* [Translation: Can you say this in Chinese?]

Child: Uhh...

Parent: *Yong Zhongwen zenme shuo?* [Translation: How do you say this in Chinese?]

Child: I don't know!

Parent: *Mama, wo xiang...* [Translation: Mummy, I want to...]

Child: (Pulls a face) *Mama, wo xiang...*

Parent: *Wo xiang he...* [Translation: I want to drink...]

Child: *He...* [Translation: Drink...]

Parent: *Sh...* [Note: This is the first syllable of *shui*, the Chinese word for "water". It's useful to use the first syllable or even just the first consonant of a word as a prompt to jog a child's memory.]

Child: *Shui!* [Translation: Water]

Parent: (Clapping and cheering) *Zai shuo yi bian - wo xiang he shui!* [Translation: Say it again – I want to have some water!]

Child: *Wo xiang he shui!* [I want to have some water!]

> ➢ This technique is grounded in the theory of "Scaffolding", theorised by the Soviet psychologist Lev Vygotsky. Vygotsky believed that when a learner is in the zone of proximal development (ZPD) for a particular task, providing the appropriate assistance will give the learner sufficient "boost" to achieve the task. The above example illustrates how this can be achieved through the use of prompts.

Some general points

- **Trust the process!**

Every child will progress at a different pace. At first, progress will probably be quite slow – don't expect them to become fluent in a week!

You're trying to change an ingrained habit, which in this case is talking to you in English. For a three-year-old child, for example, who started talking at the age of one, that's a two-year habit you're trying to change. Of course, you should expect considerable resistance. Human beings are creatures of habit, and children are no different. Fortunately, their brain is also much more malleable and elastic than ours so it will be easier for them to acquire a new habit. **There's no consensus among experts as to how long it takes to form a habit, but most agree that it's somewhere *between one and three months*[xviii].**

However, in my own experience, I saw noticeable progress actually *sooner* than I expected. Well, I expected this to take six months at least, considering Alexey pretty much did not speak any Mandarin at this point! In reality, within a week or so, Alexey started to say single words or phrases in Chinese *spontaneously*. As mentioned previously, after about three months, he was basically fluent in Chinese, which by my definition meant that he could communicate and express himself in Chinese in most situations, at an age-appropriate level. And by this time, he was also consistently addressing me in Chinese only.

A typical timeline of progression might look something like this:

BEGINNING: Can understand speech (input) in the target language, but unable to say things (output) in the target language

IMPLEMENTING "THE BOOTCAMP METHOD"

A WEEK LATER: Can repeat an utterance in the target language by copying the parent, with some difficulty. May start to use a few words/ phrases in the target language spontaneously on some occasions.

A FEW WEEKS LATER: Can repeat words and sentences by copying parent(s) with more ease. May start to use words/ phrases in the target language more and more frequently.

A MONTH OR SO LATER: Can say simple sentences in the target language, when requested by parent(s) or caregiver(s). May spontaneously use the target language with increasing frequency.

2-3 MONTHS LATER: Can spontaneously say most things in the target language, unprompted, without saying it in English first.

Obviously the exact amount of time it takes to reach each milestone will be different for each child, depending on numerous factors including:

- The child's age and level of development

- The child's temperament and aptitude

- How consistently "The Bootcamp Method" is applied

- The amount of time the parent(s)/ caregiver(s) spends talking to the child

In any case, I really recommend giving "The Bootcamp Method" two to three months, or at the very minimum, one whole month, before you decide whether or not to continue. As with any programme designed to change long-term habits – think dieting, going to the gym, quitting smoking etc. – the first couple of weeks will be the hardest and that's probably when most people give up. If you can push through to at least the one-month mark, your chance of success (actually, I should say your child's chance of success, as this is ultimately about them!) will be much higher. **And as your child begins to use the target language more and more, it should feel more rewarding and less like a chore, both for you and your child.**

70

Your child will struggle with longer sentences. If they say a long sentence in English, or a mixture of English and the target language, be patient and say it back to them in the target language, pausing several times if necessary. **The same principle applies – make them repeat the utterance, even if it's a longer sentence!** If this seems too daunting and you'd rather get your child comfortable with single words and shorter phrases first, that's fine – just be prepared to wait longer before your child becomes fluent.

When they start speaking to you spontaneously in the target language, even if it's just single words/ phrases in the beginning, **do offer plenty of praise**! This creates positive reinforcement and will encourage them to keep their efforts up. A **star chart with stickers** may also be useful in keeping motivation levels up. Feel free to experiment with different "systems" – perhaps at the beginning, every time your child says something spontaneously in the target language, they can get a sticker on their star chart; then further down the line, perhaps for every day that they speak to you exclusively in the target language, they get a big, special sticker and maybe even a prize!

- **Don't be discouraged if your child makes lots of mistakes to start with.** At the beginning of this process, my son had the tendency to translate from English to Chinese in his head (he was probably unaware of the process, of course), so longer sentences often came out a bit funny. **In my opinion, it's important to gently correct them right from the beginning.** I came to this conclusion based on my personal observation of my children. My husband almost never corrected them when he started using "The Bootcamp Method" with them. While they can both speak Russian now, they both make mistakes with cases and conjugations frequently. Obviously, even children who are native speakers of a language can make mistakes too, but our kids still habitually make quite basic mistakes when speaking Russian. My husband now corrects them more often, and they are definitely improving, but our experience really convinced me that gentle correction from early on does make a difference. But of course, **make sure corrections don't come across in a harsh way**! After all, they are doing a *great* job just by speaking the target language.

Simply repeat the sentence in the correct way, and ask them to say it back, as per the basic "Bootcamp Method". Remember, the key is to reinforce correct output. If you just give the child the correct input without ensuring they do the hard work of producing output, it's much less likely to stick.

You might be thinking – hang on, didn't I learn to speak English (or whatever your mother tongue is) in a grammatically correct way, without anyone teaching, much less correcting me? But there's a big difference between acquiring your mother tongue, or more specifically, the majority language you grew up with, versus acquiring a language mostly from just one or two individuals (i.e. your parents)! In the former case, a child acquires the language through interacting with a limitless number of different individuals, in an environment where that language is dominant. The child receives a vast amount of (mostly) grammatically correct and varied input on a daily basis. In the latter case, a child's parent may be the *only* person from whom they can acquire the target language. Of course, if your child is *already* fluent in the target language, by definition they are already getting enough exposure to the language, and you've been doing everything right. But if you're struggling to make your child speak the language, then that probably means that what you are currently doing is not sufficient, for any number of reason, and it's time to change things up.

Having said that though, please don't get too hung up on mistakes. Even speaking the target language in a "Tarzan-esque" way to begin with is a giant step in the right direction!

Example: how to gently correct a mistake

Child: *Ya khochu voda.* [Translation from Russian: I want water. The correct form of *voda*, in this sentence, should be *vodu*, the accusative form of the noun.]

Parent: *Skazhi, ya khochu vodu.* [Translation: Say, I want water. The parent basically repeats the same sentence in the grammatically correct form.]

Child: *Ya khochu vodu.*

- **Children tend to repeatedly make the same type of mistakes in the target language**, often influenced by specific features of their dominant language. For example, in English, the location word is almost always positioned at the end of a sentence, whereas in Chinese it tends to be the opposite. So for example, in English you would say: "I played football at school." In Chinese you would say the equivalent of "I at school played football."

So my son would often say things in Chinese using the English word order. I always gently correct him and I'm glad to report that he now makes a lot less mistakes. Of course, it's impossible to tell if that's mostly a result of my "corrective" technique, or a result of natural linguistic development – most likely it's a combination of the two. But as long as you keep things gentle and avoid negativity, it really can't do any harm in my opinion, and may accelerate the child's progress.

Let's say you've been using "The Bootcamp Method" for a while, and they make a mistake which has previously occurred and which you've corrected many times. Instead of "spoon-feeding" him the correct sentence, you can try to elicit the correct output by prompting the child. If you do this repeatedly, gently prompting your child to use the correct form every time, your child should eventually stop making

73

that particular mistake altogether as the correct form becomes automatic.

Example: correcting a frequently-made mistake by prompting

Child: *Ya khochu voda.* [Translation from Russian: I want water. The correct form of *voda*, in this sentence, should be *vodu*, the accusative form of the noun.]

Parent: OK. *Kak provilno skazat?* [Translation: OK. What's the correct way of saying it?]

Child: Hmm… *Ya khochu… vodu?*

Parent: *Pravilno! Molodyetz!* [Translation: Correct! Well done!]

I hope you've picked up some practical tips on how to help your child make that leap from understanding a language to actively speaking it. If you persevere, you and your child should definitely begin to see some concrete results in a matter of months.

In the next chapter, I will address some of the most common questions parents who want to raise multilingual kids may have.

CHAPTER 7

Q&AS

For some parents, raising their kids to be bilingual or multilingual is a straightforward, almost effortless process while for others, it can feel like a real struggle. In this chapter I've put together some of the most commonly asked questions parents may have, covering a range of topics from weekend language schools, to teaching your child how to read and write in the target language. To help you find the most relevant information, I've listed the questions below so you can skip to the relevant section straight away.

I've tried to implement The Bootcamp Method but my child simply refuses to reply to me in my language. What should I do?

My child mixes different languages. Should I be concerned?

Should I pretend not to understand what my child says when they use English (or whatever your majority language is)?

I'm fluent in the target language I'd like to pass on to my child but I'm not a native speaker. Can I still try to raise my child to be bilingual?

What kind of roles do TV, Youtube, and other electronic media play in a child's language development?

Is it necessary to send my child to a weekend language school?

I want my kids to learn how to read and write in our target language too. What can I do?

I am monolingual but would like my child to learn another language from a young age. What are my options?

My child is already in primary/elementary school. Is it too late to start introducing a second language?

Are bilingual children more likely to have language delays and other difficulties?

How do I deal with negative reactions from other people?

Q&As

I've tried to implement The Bootcamp Method but my child simply refuses to reply to me in my language. What should I do?

Firstly, well done on taking proactive action to help your child become fluent in the target language. I know first-hand how frustrating it can be when your child just keeps talking to you in English, despite your best efforts. This problem is extremely common and one that many parents struggle with.

It is possible that your child is just not ready yet – this is more likely if your child is very young (let's say, under two and a half/ three years old), **and/or has very limited verbal skills even in their dominant language**, in which case I wouldn't even advise using "The Bootcamp Method" in the first place. As the Chinese idiom goes, you cannot "pull up a shoot to help it grow". **However, if your child can communicate very well in their dominant language, and understands everything you say in the target language, then I'd say your child is definitely capable of speaking the target language** too, as their mental apparatus for "expressive language" (producing output) is clearly functioning normally.

If that's the case, I urge you to keep trying. Remember: habit formation takes two to three months. Also remember what I said in Chapter 1 about what that Dutch-French dad said to me – you *are* the centre of your child's world (for now!) and if they *must* speak to you in the target language in order to get your attention and/ or have their needs met, they *will* eventually do it. **The onus is on *you*, the parent, to create the *need* for them to use the language.**

This goes back to Principle Number One (see Chapter 3): The golden equation: BILINGUAL SUCCESS = EXPOSURE + NEED. **If you believe that the child is getting adequate exposure, and you're certain that you're using the target language at least 95% of the time, then the problem most likely stems from the lack of need to speak the target language from the child's perspective.** Remember, human beings are lazy! If they can get everything they need (getting mummy's/ daddy's attention; having their needs met; getting their points across) using their dominant language, why would they take the trouble to speak a much more "difficult" language?

They key with "The Bootcamp Method" is that you have to be ***gentle*** but ***firm***. **Don't shout or yell at them when they refuse to say something in the target language.** If you turn it into some sort of emotional battle, you might just awaken the little rebel in your kid – this is especially true for very strong-willed children. It's a battle you can't win! Be calm (I know, it's sometimes easier said than done) and **simply ask them to repeat what they've just said in the target language**. If they can't say it, say it for them and ask them to repeat it. If they want something (say, a cup of water), do not fulfil the request until they've successfully said the required word or sentence in the target language, even if they're just repeating after you.

I know it sounds a bit extreme but trust me – it will work if you stick with it and do it *consistently*. It is no more extreme or cruel than sleep-training your child using some sort of "Cry it Out" method, and many (if not most!) parents I know have sleep-trained their child in the quest for better sleep. Nevertheless, I hope it goes without saying that **if your child is in distress, in pain or in danger in any way, attending to their needs will take precedence over language "training"!**

77

Another thing to bear in mind is that the first few weeks will inevitably be the hardest and if you can push through the early frustrating stage, it should get easier. Once fluency is established, conversing with your child in the target language should become an enjoyable and rewarding experience for you both.

You may struggle with feelings of guilt during the "training" process. Am I a bad parent for making my child do something they're reluctant to do? Am I being a pushy Tiger Mum (or Dad)? Is my child gonna *hate* me? **One thing worth pointing out is that this is actually harder work for *you* than for your child!** You are helping your child acquire an extremely useful skill and reap all the potential benefits of being bilingual or multilingual; keep it up and be assured that they will thank you for it one day.

My Child Mixes Different Languages. Should I Be Concerned?

Most, if not all, children who speak more than one language do mix languages. The technical term for this is "code mixing", and it's a totally normal part of language acquisition – it is not a sign of "confusion" but is in fact a sign of creativity and problem solving. Your child is learning to compensate for the vocabulary they lack in one language by incorporating words from another language. You'll notice that as your child gets older, the amount of mixing will gradually decrease; this is because as their vocabulary size in each language grows, they won't have the *need* to mix anymore.

My own children did a lot of mixing when they were very little – one of my favourite examples is when my daughter, aged two at the time, said: "*Gege boom ya!*" Translation: "Gege" is the Chinese word for "older brother"; "boom" is her own word (or an English sound-word?) meaning "to bump into"; "ya" is the Russian word for "I", but with the incorrect case ending. I know; it's pretty hilarious. While both my children still mix their languages occasionally, it happens far less frequently now.

So what *should* you do when your child mixes their languages? Firstly, give yourself permission to relax and **accept that code mixing is normal**. It is usually just a phase that they'll grow out of, as their vocabulary sizes in each of their languages grow. **Continue to give your child adequate exposure to the target language(s) to help them expand their vocabulary.**

If your child is actively trying to speak the target language with you but is incorporating words from the majority language, I would avoid making the child repeat everything "correctly" (as you normally would during the "Bootcamp Method" training process) because they're already doing a great job by trying to speak the target language and you don't want to discourage them. In this case, I suggest "modelling" the correct language for the child: **when they mix languages, repeat what they *should* say in the target language.** This way, your child still gets the correct input without feeling discouraged – the last thing you want is for your child to lose their confidence to speak the target language! However, if the mixing gets worse and not better over time, stricter measures may be necessary.

Another thing to be mindful of is the extent to which *you* yourself mix your languages. We adults are just as guilty of this as the little ones! Of course mixing languages is not a problem in itself; in many countries it's the cultural norm to mix languages with abandon. My husband was rather impressed when he was in Moldova once and saw how the locals constantly and seamlessly switched between Russian, Moldovan and the local dialect; and no one seemed in the least confused! But when you're trying to pass on a minority language to your child, this is not an approach I would recommend. Around the same time that I started implementing "The Bootcamp Method" with my children, I also became a lot more aware of how many English words I was using in my supposedly Chinese sentences, and had to really make a conscious decision to minimise such mixing. So next time you catch yourself using non-target-language words in your sentences while you're talking to your child, make a mental note of it and try to say it again with the "right" word in the target language!

Should I Pretend Not To Understand What My Child Says When They Use English (Or Whatever Your Majority Language Is)?

To pretend, or not to be pretend? That is the question…

Now, I know this is a tactic favoured by some experts, and anecdotally recommended by lots of parents who have successfully raised bilingual kids. However, it is not a tactic I use or would recommend for a number of reasons.

Firstly, the claim that you "don't understand English" simply isn't very believable from your child's perspective, and is therefore potentially confusing to your child. Look at it this way: you live in a country where the majority language is English (or whichever language is applicable) and you cannot possibly avoid speaking English in front of your child at some point, if only to have a chat with other parents at the school gate. So your child knows for a fact that you can speak English. Personally I don't think it's sending out a very good message when you tell your child something that they know is blatantly untrue. Of course, many parents would disagree with me on this, and many would say that it's worked for them; at the end of the day, it's your decision. But rather than saying, "I don't understand English," or "I don't understand what you're saying", **in my opinion it's better and just as effective to say: "Did you mean to say… ["Translate" what they just said in English into the target language]?" This way you show that you're trying to help them; that you're working with them.** It models a collaborative and more equal relationship between parent and child, which I think is healthier.

Secondly, as a parent, I strongly believe that your emotional connection to your child should trump any educational imperatives. **It can be hurtful to a child when their mum or dad (or other caregivers) simply dismisses their needs or desires to express themselves by saying "I don't understand", especially when they clearly do! My advice therefore is to always acknowledge what your child says, but to also prompt and encourage them to use the target language at all times,** as per "The Bootcamp Method".

Having said that, if everything else has failed, by all means give the "I-don't- understand-English" strategy a try. It has worked for many parents and it may well work for you.

I'm Fluent In The Target Language I'd Like To Pass On To My Child But I'm Not A Native Speaker. Can I Still Try To Raise My Child To Be Bilingual?

My answer is a resounding *Yes*! Again, many experts would disagree with me on this. The prevailing wisdom is that you should always speak to your child in your most proficient language, which is usually your mother tongue. However, I personally do not support this "purist" approach. Maybe I'm biased – I switched from Cantonese (my "mother tongue", although not necessarily my most proficient language) to Mandarin with my own kids. But if you're genuinely fluent in the target language – again, there are so many definitions of "fluency" that the whole concept is very fuzzy – there's absolutely no reason why you can't speak to your child in this language. **The purpose of language is ultimately effective communication. If you're fluent enough to achieve that, you are fluent enough to speak it with your child.**

81

OK, your child's accent may not be perfect – I'll be the first to admit that my children definitely have a bit of a funny accent when they speak Mandarin (*and* English, *and* Russian!) – but is it not better to speak a language fluently with a slight accent, than not to be able to speak it at all? Would you tell an adult learner that it's pointless trying to learn a language because he will never sound like a native speaker? Almost all of my non-British-born friends and acquaintances, most of whom are highly-skilled professionals working in the UK, have a slight "foreign" accent. So in my opinion, **having an accent certainly doesn't mean you're not fluent in a language**. And for children, such accents will most *not* be permanent anyway. So many parents have told me how their children acquired an perfect native accent after spending a summer in their parents'/ grandparents' hometown! So my point is this: **focus on fluency, and don't sweat over relatively minor details like accent.**

However, if you're trying to raise your child to be fluent in a language which may not be your most proficient language for whatever reason – maybe it's not your mother tongue, or maybe you've lived in another country for a very long time and hardly ever get to use your first language – **it's important to improve or at least maintain your own proficiency in the target language as much as possible**. As a Mandarin tutor and translator, I have to use Mandarin for work on a daily basis but I still at times feel that my vocabulary is insufficient. And the language I use with the kids is very different from the kind of language I use when I translate a piece of news article, for example! Since reading Annika Bourgogne's highly informative book *Be Bilingual – Practical Ideas for Multilingual Families*, which offers excellent advice for parents in this type of situation, I've implemented a few changes in my own life to improve my Mandarin. Here are a few "hacks" that you could try to boost your fluency in the target language:

> ➤ **Spend some time reading a book in the target language every day.** As any expert would tell you, there is no better

way to improve your vocabulary in any language than reading. I am an avid reader myself and read for leisure every evening once the kids are in bed. I now make sure that I spend half of that time reading a Chinese book. This relatively small adjustment has given my vocabulary a huge boost. I would also recommend downloading a dictionary App on your phone so you can look up words easily. Most dictionary Apps now enable you to create vocabulary flashcards, which you can review regularly. Keep doing this for a while and your confidence in using the target language will certainly grow alongside your vocabulary!

➤ **Change the default language on your computer to the target language.** This is a small change that can make quite a big difference to your exposure to the target language, as most of us spend so much time on our computers these days. Of course you can or even should do the same on your smartphone, but just make sure you can still drive safely when Google Maps starts speaking to you in the target language! I learnt this the hard way while driving to the supermarket with the kids one day – I had to pull over in a panic and eventually admitted defeat and changed the default language back to English. But if road safety is not an issue, changing the default language on your phone is really a no-brainer.

➤ **Read or listen to the news in the target language during breaks.** Many of us like to catch up on the news on our phones or computers at lunchtime (or maybe even throughout the day). So why not download a news App in the target language? Or watch news videos in the target language on Youtube? Even 10-15 minutes a day can give your reading and listening skills a real boost.

➤ **Enjoy entertainment in the target language during your "me-time".** Do you have a guilty pleasure? Perhaps it's watching music videos, playing video games, or perhaps even binge-watching trashy reality TV shows? It's okay, we all need to unwind after (or even during) a long day! A quick confession: my guilty pleasure is watching makeup tutorials on Youtube. So now, rather than watching such videos in English, I just look for similar content in Chinese. People learn languages much better through content that's interesting to them individually. The technical word for this is "compelling content". So seek out content in the target language that's of interest to you, and effortlessly improve your language skills while enjoying your precious me-time.

Also, for parents in this situation, I highly recommend checking out the Chalk Academy (www.chalkacademy.com) website (more on this in Chapter 9), where a third-generation Chinese-American mum shares her experience of raising trilingual children as a non-fluent speaker. I also know parents in real life who are raising their children to be fluent in a language that's not their own mother tongue. Below are two real-life examples I'd like to share with you.

Case study 1

I once met a little girl at our local library, who was conversing with a Chinese nanny in Mandarin. The nanny and I started chatting and what she told me was truly eye-opening – the little girl was the daughter of a local politician of South Asian origins, who was married to an Englishman. The mother spoke to the child in her native language, and the English father spoke to her in … Mandarin! He learned the language as an adult and became fluent after spending some time in China. He was determined to raise his daughter to be trilingual and started speaking to her in Mandarin exclusively from birth. The nanny was also technically a non-native speaker – like me, she's a Hong Konger who is fluent in Mandarin. From my brief interaction with the little girl, I would say that while her Chinese wasn't "perfect", she could certainly express herself adequately for her age. It just shows that you do not have to be native speaker of the target language to succeed. What you *do* need is lots of determination.

Case study 2

When my daughter was still a baby, I met a mum at a local baby group, who always spoke to her daughter in Spanish. I always assumed that the mum was Spanish but when I bumped into her again at my daughter's nursery one day (turns out the two girls were friends at nursery!), I found out that she's fully British born-and-bred, and so is her husband! In a subsequent conversation, she told me that she came from a very small English town where everyone only spoke English. She studied Spanish at university and spent lots of time in Spain. Being fluent in the language, and now living in a wonderfully cosmopolitan part of London, she thought it'd be a great idea to raise her daughter to be bilingual. I asked her if she sometimes found it challenging and she said that yes, there were times when she wasn't sure what a word was in Spanish but on the whole she still thought it was do-able and certainly rewarding; she was absolutely convinced that the potential benefits (her daughter being able to communicate in Spanish) far outweighed the negatives (that her daughter might not speak like a native speaker; the amount of effort required on the mother's part etc.). And once her daughter was a bit older, she said, it could be fun to look words up together! If this mum can do it, with a positive can-do attitude and determination, so can you. And if you're trying to pass on your mother tongue to your child – well, you really have zero excuse not to do it!

What Kind Of Roles Do TV, Youtube, And Other Electronic Media Play In A Child's Language Development?

You often hear about people who claim to have learned to speak a language just by watching TV. Of course, it is not impossible but it's certainly not an approach I (or any expert) would recommend for the average adult learner, much less a child. One thing that all linguists agree on is **that language acquisition requires some form of two-way interaction. And for a young child, this means one-on-one interaction with a small number of key caregivers, usually including their parents.**

Of course, as long as this condition is met, electronic media in the target language *can* be a useful supplementary tool in that it provides engaging, stimulating linguistic input for the child. However, these resources can never replace real-life interaction with an actual human being. Once they are older, it's possible to replace some of that real-life interaction with Skype lessons or video chats, but the key is still **two-way interaction. If you (assuming you're the parent) are too busy to give your child lots of two-way interaction, and sending your child to a bilingual nursery/ school is not an option, you'll have to find a babysitter, nanny, childminder or grandparent (if you're lucky) who can spend a significant amount of time with your child, speaking in the target language, in order to give them enough exposure to the target language.** And make sure this caregiver does not just put your child in front of a screen all day!

In our household, my husband has subscribed to a Russian TV service to enable us to watch Russian programmes on a normal TV set. Lots of multilingual families I know have a similar set-up so it's definitely worth investigating these options for your target language in your country of residence. The Disney+ Channel is also a popular subscription service for families – their legacy content is available in English, French, Dutch and Spanish, while Disney+ Original content is available in up to 16 languages, which is fantastic for multilingual families out there.

Needless to say, there are literally countless kids' programmes on the internet and Youtube – you are bound to find something suitable in your target language. *Peppa Pig* in Mandarin is a big hit with our kids!

During lockdown, I unfortunately had to put my kids in front of the TV way too much but knowing that they were at least gaining some exposure to one of our target languages assuaged the parental guilt somewhat.

In Chapter 9, you can see a list of useful websites with online language resources for children that may be of interest.

Is It Necessary To Send My Child To A Weekend Language School?

OK, I have *a lot* to say on this topic as both of my children attend Russian school every Saturday during term-time, and my son used to go to Chinese school on Sundays too, before the pandemic hit. Another reason we stopped sending Alexey to Chinese school is that since I implemented The Bootcamp Method, his Mandarin had improved so much that by the time the first lockdown started, he was already speaking more Chinese than most, if not all, the other kids in his class, so we decided there was no point carrying on especially with online-only lessons.

Despite all this, my answer to this question is a definite no. **It is not necessary to send your child to a weekend language school, although it may be helpful, depending on: 1) the school itself; 2) what you're hoping to achieve**. Let me explain.

Weekend schools such as the ones we've sent our kids to can vary considerably in terms of the kind of families who send their children there, and in terms of their primary purposes. The Chinese school Alexey went to, for example, attracted many families with one parent of Chinese heritage (and this parent wasn't necessarily a Chinese speaker), as well as a significantly number of families with no connection to China or the Chinese language at all. As a result, from my own observation, the majority of children who attended this school do not speak Chinese fluently, or use the language in a significant way at home. Their classes are a good way to introduce the children to the language and give them some exposure. But for a significant proportion of these children, for whom the two-hour weekly classes are more or less their only sources of exposure to the language, the chances of achieving fluency are sadly quite slim. **Schools like this one are still beneficial in terms of providing extra-curricular activities and enrichment (and weekend childcare for the parents!), but are unlikely to help your child become fluent in your target language on their own.** In fact, if you already provide significant exposure to the target language at home, and practise something like The Bootcamp Method, you may find that such schools add too little value to your child's linguistic development to justify the expenses.

In contrast, the Russian school our kids attend is quite different in that every single family there has at least one Russian-speaking parent. In Alexey's class, a significant proportion of the children are already fully bilingual in English and Russian (and maybe even a third language). This school caters for children of all ages, from age two all the way up to A-Level. From what I've seen, all the older children there are fully bilingual and almost always converse in Russian among themselves outside of the classroom, which I didn't expect!

Our son actually started attending this school just after he turned two (he was still in nappies) at my husband's insistence. And in all honesty (I better hide this section from my husband), I think the first year was a bit of a waste of time and money in terms of language-acquisition benefits. Yes, our son enjoyed the classes as an extra-curricular activity and it was something for us to do on the weekend, but his Russian improved very little. For Alexey, the two real turning points were: 1) My husband adopting a less strict version of The Bootcamp Method when Alexey was just over three years old, at the same time as I did; 2) when my husband started working from home during the first national lockdown and spending more time with him during the week. Once again, this demonstrates the paramount importance of *regular* exposure and *one-on-one interaction.*

Now that my son has been attending this school for nearly three years, and my daughter for just under a year, I can really see the benefits of these weekly lessons, especially when it comes to helping the kids develop their Russian literacy skills. The teachers are very good at teaching the alphabet in an engaging way, and they set us homework to do at home, which my husband does with both kids on most days. Of course, if you have the time and patience, it's possible to do all this yourself – **I highly recommend Adam Beck's excellent book *Maximize Your Child's Bilingual Ability: Ideas and inspiration for even greater success and joy raising bilingual kids* for ideas on how to do teach your child literacy skills in the target language, without sending your kids to a bilingual school or even a weekend school. The key is to establish good routines and stick with them. The three daily routines Beck recommends and uses with his own kids are: 1) Reading a book aloud at breakfast; 2) Frequent interaction; 3) Having a homework routine in the evening.** You may not have the time to read a book at breakfast and that's okay – bedtime can be just as good! The point is to establish solid routines, and stick to them.

So the bottom line is, **if your child already speaks the target language with some fluency, weekend language schools are optional. If your goal is to help your child develop good literacy skills in the target language, weekend classes can be useful but only if you choose a school targeted at children who are already fluent**. But if, on the other hand, money is no object (and some of these schools can be really expensive), and you don't mind ferrying your child to and from the school, of course it won't hurt! **Just don't expect your child to become fluent in the target language purely through weekend classes, if the home environment and formal education environment do not provide sufficient language exposure.**

89

Case study 3

One of Alexey's former nursery friends has a Cantonese-speaking mother and a French father. The mum and I became friends and she told me that her son can understand Cantonese but can't speak it, and she's come to accept that. Her son is, however, perfectly bilingual in French and English and I asked her if her son goes to a French language school on the weekend. She chuckled and told me that no, it's all down to her very patient husband, who spends lots of time talking to him and, crucially, reading with him in French *every evening*. She, on the other hand, just doesn't have the patience! They also often spend weeks at a time in France, which really helps provide immersion in the target language.

So if you have the patience to sit down with your child every day and read a few books together in your target language, you might be surprised by how quickly your child's fluency improves!

I Want My Kids To Learn How To Read And Write In Our Target Language Too. What Can We Do?

There are different schools of thought on the relative roles of fluency and literacy in a child's language development. In his book *Trilingual by Six: The Sane Way to Raise Intelligent, Talented Children*, Lennis Dippel emphasises the differences between these two skills: **while *fluency* is rooted in the human biological instinct of speech, *literacy* is a cultural skill that has to be learned**. As such, he argues that it's important to establish oral fluency early on, in early childhood, while the "language acquisition device" – the instinctive mental capacity which enables an infant to acquire and produce language, as theorised by Noam Chomsky – is in optimal operational mode. Literacy, on the other hand, can reasonably wait till the school years.

In contrast, the author Adam Beck, in his book *Maximize Your Child's Bilingual Ability*, makes a convincing case for the argument that **literacy actually helps improve fluency, in the same way that a well-read person tends to be well-spoken**, as reading provides the child's developing brain with a framework of sophisticated language. In his own case – his children are fully bilingual and biliterate in English and Japanese – as the scripts of the family's two languages are so radically different, he decided to introduce reading and writing very early on, as soon as his children could hold a pen properly. As a general rule, he thinks **age three or four is a good time to introduce reading and writing in the target language, ideally before the child learns to read and write in the majority language. But even from birth, reading should play a big role on a daily basis as it enriches the child's vocabulary and grammar with sophisticated language.**

As this book is primarily concerned with oral fluency and the years of early childhood, and on a personal level, my own children are only at the very early stages of literacy acquisition in all three of their languages, my focus for the time being will be on speaking and listening.

Having said that, it's always a good idea to introduce literacy basics such as the alphabet (or in the case of Chinese, some simple ideograms) **in your target language early on, at about the same time as you or the child's nursery/ school introduces the alphabet of the majority language.**

If a high level of literacy is your goal, be ready to invest a lot of time towards achieving this goal, as your child will most likely receive very little, if any reinforcement in reading and writing the target language in the formal education system (unless you send your child to a school with a fully bilingual curriculum).

It's worth repeating that from the baby months, **you should already be spending lots of time reading with your child in the target**

language on a daily basis – aim for 15 minutes a day as a realistic target. The more the better – you can never read too much! At this stage, of course, it's all about laying the foundation for literacy rather than teaching the child actual reading and writing. If you don't have access to books written in your target language, do not fret! **Just grab any picture books and talk to your child about what you see.** They will love hearing your voice and will be expanding their vocabulary. Once they can start speaking, ask them questions about things in the book and encourage them to talk about the pictures, even if it's just single words at this stage.

Between ages two and three, it's a good idea to introduce the writing system of your target language in a gentle way. This is especially important if the writing system of the target language is very different from that of the majority language. At this stage, the main goal is to stimulate their interest in this writing system, and create a sense of familiarity.

It's absolutely possible to teach your child to read and write in the target language yourself, of course, but it will require a significant amount of parental investment in terms of time, effort and patience. **If you're pursuing the "DIY" route, then once again I recommend establishing and sticking with the daily routines of reading and homework**. I explained this in some detail under the section "Principle 5: Establish useful routines and stick to them" from Chapter 3 of this book, but here's a quick summary:

- **Introduce a literacy learning routine.** Start with a 10- or 15-minute session per day, and ideally this routine should take place at the same time every day.
- Childhood development experts generally agree that **a reasonable attention span to expect of a child is two to three minutes per year of their age**, so take this into account when planning your routine to minimise frustration.

- In terms of learning materials, some visually attractive worksheets or even language textbooks could be very useful but are *not* essential. **All you really need is a notepad and some pens!**

- **Each session should begin with reviewing some vocabulary that's already been covered.** In fact, as much as one third of your session should be focused on reviewing previous learning – I won't go into the details of the science here but it is generally thought that a learner has to be exposed to a word anything between 6 to 17 times before the word is committed to the learner's long-term memory.

- As soon as your child is able to, **encourage them to read sentences aloud,** however slowly and imperfectly. It will give them a real confidence boost and keep motivation levels up!

- **Encourage your child to practise writing as much as possible.** Even if they can only produce doodles at this stage, the fine motor skill practice will prove invaluable for future literacy learning.

- **Do your best to stick to this routine on most days.** However, if you're really short on time on any given day, try to squeeze in two minutes (or even just one minute!) reviewing previous learning. This will reinforce the idea that "I have to sit down and study [the target language] every day" in your child's mind and make it easier persevere in the long term.

In real life, most parents I know whose older children have attained a high level of literacy in their target language achieved this goal with the help of weekend language schools and/or private tutors. **If you are really committed to helping your child achieve a high level of literacy in the target language,** perhaps because you're considering re-locating to another country or transitioning your child to a different schooling system, **your best bet would probably be to send your child to a fully bilingual school from a young age.** This is probably the most costly but equally the most foolproof method.

Nevertheless, always remember that as a parent, you can achieve so much without additional expenses and outside help, as long as you have the time and patience to sit down with your child and teach them how to read and write in the target language, and are able to keep this up over the course of many years. It is certainly achievable for any parent, so don't let anyone tell you otherwise!

I Am Monolingual But Would Like My Child To Learn Another Language From A Young Age. What Are My Options?

While raising your child to be bilingual when you're a native speaker of the target language can be difficult enough, the challenge will inevitably be far greater for those parents who are monolingual. However, it's certainly an achievable goal but will take some extra planning, perhaps before the child is even born! Ultimately, the rewards for your child will make all the effort worthwhile.

As discussed previously, two major factors will determine how readily your child will acquire the target language: 1) How early you start introducing the target language; 2) How much exposure to the target language the child receives, especially in the form of one-on-one, two-way interaction.

To maximise your chance of success, **consider hiring a nanny, au-pair or babysitter who will speak to your child exclusively in the target language before your child turns three.** Again, the earlier the better, and the more days that caregiver can spend with your child, the better. For example, three hours per day, five days a week is probably preferable to 15 hours spread over two days. The reason is that, when it comes to language acquisition, or in fact the acquisition of any other skill, frequent practice and exposure is key as it creates constant reinforcement in the brain. **It is often cited that a child needs to be exposed to a language 30% of their waking time to become fluent in the language.** There's no actual scientific evidence to back this up, but this "30% rule" is still a pretty useful guideline. **That works out to be approximately 25 hours a week,** depending on the child's schedule. I know that figure may or may not be achievable, depending on your personal circumstances, but it's still a useful figure to keep in mind.

Once your child is ready to start school, you should seriously consider enrolling them in a fully bilingual school in order to get maximum exposure to the target language. If that's not an option, having an after-school nanny for two to three hours a day, supplemented by weekend classes, would still give your child an excellent chance of success.

If possible, try to befriend other families in your area who speak your target language and arrange play-dates and other activities with them. **Interacting with children who speak the target language is extremely beneficial for your child as children learn best through play, and especially through playing with their peers**. When my daughter Alina started nursery shortly before she turned two, I was unsure how much English she understood or spoke, as we only spoke Chinese when we were together. But soon after she started nursery it became evident that she'd picked it up very, very quickly, through interacting with her new friends and nursery staff. In Chapter 5, under the "Step 5: Find Support" section, I offer some ideas on how to find support in your local area; in Chapter 9, you'll also find some websites with resources for multilingual families that may be of interest.

At home, books, videos and other materials in the target language can all help create a rich linguistic environment. In Chapter 9, you'll find ways to help you locate these resources. **If at all possible, take your child to a country where the target language is the majority language**. Nothing will bring a language to life more than being surrounded by people living their lives in that language!

Above all, ignore the naysayers who tell you it's a waste of time and/or money (although I suspect you'll meet far more people who are in awe of your determination!). Focus on your goals and keep your eye on the prize: with good planning, hard work and perseverance, your child *can* and *will* reap the benefits of bilingualism.

My Child Is Already In Primary/Elementary School. Is It Too Late To Start Introducing A Second Language?

Assuming you and/or your partner is a native speaker, or a highly proficient speaker of the target language you'd like your child to acquire, no, it's not too late. Although most experts agree that, generally speaking, the earlier you start, the better, there's no consensus on the exact age threshold for achieving native-like fluency in a language. **Evidence suggests that up to the age of about 10, given the right conditions and environment, a child can still learn a language from scratch and achieve native-level fluency with no noticeable accent. And if your expectations are slightly lower, meaning that you simply want your child to be fluent in the target language, but not necessarily acquire a native-like accent and proficiency, then your chances of success should be really good.**

One of my students – a seventeen-year old boy in Year 12 – moved to the UK from his native Russia at the age of 10 with practically zero English. He now speaks perfect English with a rather posh North-London accent although, interestingly, he still considers Russian to be his first language. My husband's twin brothers moved to Australia from Russia at the age of seven with zero English, but now both consider English to be their first language. Of course, in both cases, the child moved to a country where the new language is dominant, which automatically created the two key conditions for language acquisition: *need* and *exposure*. So your situation will not be comparable, unless your family moves to a country where the target language is the majority language. However, my point is that your child's chance of success is still very good, even in the primary-school years, given you can maximise your child's need to speak the target language, and their exposure to the language.

So if your child already has a passive knowledge of the target language but cannot speak it, start putting The Bootcamp Method into practice *today*. The older your child is, the more resistant they are likely to be so you may need to take a more gradual approach and be extra patient. So instead of asking your child to repeat whole sentences in the target language, as per the standard Bootcamp Method, perhaps start with single words and common phrases, and gradually work your way up to full sentences.

On the other hand, if you never, or rarely spoke to your child in the target language before, start introducing it now. Again, the older your child is, the more gradual your approach might need to be. **The "Time and Place" strategy (see Chapter 4) could be a great way to start.** For example, start talking to them in the target language in certain settings – at dinnertime, on family days out etc.; then gradually increase the percentage of time using the target language to something close to 100%. Once the child achieves a good level of passive knowledge – meaning that they understand most of what you say in the target language – start implementing The Bootcamp Method.

All the tips offered in previous chapters relating to the reinforcement of the target language apply here: books, audio-visual materials, Skype chat, nannies/ au pairs/ babysitters, socialising with other families who speak your target language, and so forth. **Does your child have any special hobbies? You can try to introduce a linguistic element to some of these hobbies.** For example, if your child enjoys videos games, perhaps you could buy a selection of new games in the target language? Or if your child already takes regular piano lessons, how about finding a piano teacher who would give lessons in the target language?

Since your child is a bit older, appeal to their sense of pride and ego. Tell them how amazing, how cool it is to be fluent in another language! Are any of their favourite celebrities or Youtubers bilingual? (On my website www.multilingualfamilyhub.com, you can find an article about multilingual celebs) Or maybe some of their friends are fluent in more than one language? This could be a great opportunity to find out more about your child's social life and interests.

Are Bilingual Children More Likely To Have Language Delays And Other Difficulties?

This is probably one of the most common misconceptions about bilingualism. Even parents of bilingual children themselves often feel that their child is somewhat "behind" due to being raised bilingual/ multilingual but **the science is very clear: bilingual children are *not* more likely than monolingual children to experience difficulties with language, to show delays in learning, or to be diagnosed with a language disorder**[xix].

I certainly felt (and sometimes still do feel) that way about my own children, especially my firstborn. He seemed to start talking a bit later than his monolingual peers and even now, almost aged five, his English vocabulary seems to be somewhat smaller than that of a typical monolingual child of the same age. So is this a sign of language delay?

Experts in bilingualism use two different measures for children's vocabulary size. "Conceptual vocabulary" is the sum of how many concepts a child knows, regardless of the language in which

the concept is known. For example, if a child knows the words chien and dog, using conceptual vocabulary scoring, these words are counted as a single word. **In contrast, "total vocabulary" is the sum of all the words known in all the languages by the child.** Using the same example, if a child knows dog and chien, these two words are counted as two words under this scoring system.

The current research on this subject suggests that young bilingual children (most if not all studies have been done on bilingual children, but presumably the same principle would apply to trilingual/ multilingual children) **do tend to have a smaller conceptual vocabulary than their monolingual peers; however, their total vocabulary tends to be larger[xx].**

To see how this works in real life, let's use an example. Mateo is a five-year-old Spanish/ English bilingual child. He knows approximately 7,000 English words, and all the equivalent Spanish words. His monolingual school-friend Jayden knows approximately 10,000 English words, which is typical for a five-year-old child. Using the "conceptual vocabulary" measure, Mateo has a vocabulary size of 7,000 words, while Jayden has 10,000 words. It's not difficult to see why Jayden's speech might seem quite a bit more advanced and sophisticated compared to that of Mateo, when you look at they way they converse in English.

However, Mateo's total vocabulary size is actually 14,000 words, when you add up all the words he knows across English and Spanish. By this measure, he has a clear advantage over his monolingual peer. When it comes to the question as to which measure is more appropriate for measuring a bilingual's child lexical abilities, experts seem to be divided right down the middle, with no clear consensus.

The reason I discussed the issue of vocabulary size at some length is that numerous studies have shown that a child's vocabulary size in infancy is a strong predictor of academic success [xxi]; parents of bilingual children may reasonably feel anxious about the effect bilingualism may have on their child when it comes to their vocabulary size. Even though this is a book about raising multilingual children, as a parent I can totally understand these concerns. Parents of bilingual/ multilingual children will be reassured to know that there's evidence to suggest that bilingual children do catch up to their monolingual peers in terms of conceptual vocabulary size as they progress through the school years[xxii]. In any case, vocabulary size is only *one* factor that correlates with academic success; natural intelligence, socioeconomic status and other factors are just as crucial.

In short, parents should absolutely not worry that being bilingual or multilingual might have a detrimental effect on their child's academic achievement. In fact, contemporary research shows that bilingual pupils are often equipped with many unique strengths that can contribute to academic success. For example, research has shown that bilingual students usually have stronger working memories and attention spans. They also outperform monolingual students on tasks that require "executive control" – this refers to self-discipline, perseverance, and other skills that help students achieve their goals. When combined with the higher abstract thinking skills these students develop, bilingual students often have the intellect and motivation to take on complex school assignments[xxiii].

However, just like some monolingual children *do* have a genuine language delay or disorder, a similar proportion of bilingual/ multilingual children will have a language delay or disorder. There is no evidence to suggest that this proportion is higher in the latter group[xxiv]. So what are the signs to look out for? According to Kidshealth.org, here are some red flags to watch for:

- By 12 months: isn't using gestures, such as pointing or waving bye-bye
- By 18 months: prefers gestures over vocalizations to communicate

- By 18 months: has trouble imitating sounds
- Has trouble understanding simple verbal requests
- By 2 years: can only imitate speech or actions; doesn't produce words or phrases spontaneously
- By 2 years: says only some sounds or words repeatedly and can't use oral language to communicate more than their immediate needs
- By 2 years: can't follow simple directions
- By 2 years: has an unusual tone of voice (such as raspy or nasal sounding)

Also contact a specialist if your child's speech is harder to understand than expected for their age:

- Parents and regular caregivers should understand about 50% of a child's speech at 2 years and 75% of it at 3 years.
- By 4 years old, a child should be mostly understood, even by people who don't know the child.

How Do I Deal With Negative Reactions From Other People?

Thankfully, attitudes towards bilingualism/ multilingualism in the western world have moved on from even just a generation ago, as most of the myths surrounding the subject have been debunked by experts in the field, aided by advances in research. My father-in-law, whose youngest son Maxim was born in Sydney, Australia in the early 2000s, once told me how teachers at Maxim's school strongly *dis*couraged them from speaking Russian at home as, in their view, having two languages was causing "confusion" and had a negative impact on his communication skills as well as development. To my father-in-law's credit, he ignored their well-meaning advice and continued to raise Maxim to be bilingual, even sending him to a weekend Russian school throughout his school years. Now in his first year of university, Maxim is fully bilingual and biliterate in English and Russian, and has always excelled academically.

In my personal experience, since I had my first child nearly five years ago, I have not received even one negative comment about my attempt to raise my children with three languages. In fact, without exception, people have been incredibly supportive! However, this may not be the case for everybody. In his book *Maximize your Child's Bilingual Ability*, Adam Beck recounts how some acquaintances have reacted negatively to his decision to speak to his children in English at all times. The fact that Japan is a highly homogenous society where a significant proportion of the population has had little exposure to foreigners may partly explain why the author encountered such reactions.

To help you understand and deal with such reactions, let's consider why some people may react in this way. In my view, there are three main reasons why people react negatively towards bilingualism: 1) they may simply feel uncomfortable being around people who speak a different language in their presence; 2) influenced by the various negative myths about bilingualism, they may have genuine concerns about the child's development and wellbeing; 3) they may unconsciously feel envious about your child's bilingual ability, which leads to feelings of inadequacy and resentment, which in turn manifest themselves as criticism of your effort; 4) a combination of the above.

So, what's the best way to deal with such reactions? Of course, you shouldn't *have* to justify your parenting decisions to other people but it might be wise to **acknowledge that person's concerns politely, before offering a brief explanation of why you're trying to raise your child to be bilingual. In most cases, the simple explanation that your child needs to learn the target language in order to communicate with relatives should suffice.** After that, feel free to just carry on as normal!

But what if the objections came from the child's school or other official authorities? These objections cannot and should not be dismissed out of hand. If that's the case, you may need to sit down for a proper chat with the relevant person-in-charge and find out if there may be genuine reasons for their concerns.

Is your child falling behind with schoolwork? Are their communication and social skills not progressing as expected? Once you've established what their concerns are, reassure them that you're doing everything to support your child's learning and development at home; however, they **shouldn't pressure you into giving up on raising your child to be bilingual. Study after study has shown that being raised with more than one language does *not* negatively affect a child's development and academic achievement**. So unless there's reason to think that your child may genuinely have speech delay issues, in which case you will need to consult a speech specialist, do not let anyone tell you that you're "confusing" your child or hampering their development by raising them with more than one language. Quite the opposite is true!

I hope this section has answered some of your questions about raising bilingual/ multilingual children. If you have any other questions that have not been covered here, feel free to leave a post on my website or email me directly. I will do my best to answer your questions.

In the next chapter, I've put together some activity ideas that will keep the little ones entertained *and* help them acquire the target language in a fun, natural way. And best of all, most of them are free and do not require fancy equipment!

CHAPTER 8

ACTIVITIES FOR MULTILINGUAL FAMILIES

In this chapter, I've put together some fun and easy activity ideas for multilingual families, whether your child is a newborn baby or already attends school. Most of the activities I've listed do not cost a penny but they do take some time and patience! **Just remember that every time you do an activity with your child in the target language, your child is taking a step forward towards better fluency.** And in this day and age, when we parents are too often distracted by emails, mobile phones, and various other demands of daily life, sitting down and getting stuck into a fun activity with your kids for 10 minutes can actually do all of us a lot of good.

So, take some time out, put your devices down, take some inspiration from the ideas in this chapter, and spend some quality time with your little one!

Newborn—Age 2

- **Sing nursery rhymes to your baby or toddler in the target language**

This is such an obvious one but singing nursery rhymes really is the single most beneficial thing you can do for a baby in terms of language development, not to mention the wonderful benefits it brings in terms of strengthening the parent-and-child bond. Your child will love hearing the sound of your voice, and they will enjoy the lovely mishmash of sounds and words, even if their comprehension is rather limited at this stage.

Use your best "baby voice" – **scientists have proved that babies respond best to that high-pitched "baby voice", known as "motherese", instinctively adopted by many parents xxv . If possible, incorporate movements and actions** to make it even more fun for the baby (and you!). The book Playsongs: Action Songs and Rhymes for Babies and Toddlers by Sheena Roberts includes lots of such "action songs" and is accompanied by a CD too.

If you're in the UK, check out your local library for "Rhyme Time" sessions targeted at very young children. Your local children's centre should have "Stay and Play" sessions too, which will give you lots of opportunity to learn such "action songs" and have fun with your baby. These council-run activities should be free for all residents. If you're looking for paid classes, Gymboree runs very good classes for young children which incorporate singing, dancing and plenty of action.

- **Read picture books together**

The benefits of reading with your child cannot be over-emphasised – there's simply no better way to help your child expand their vocabulary and to develop a love for language. As I said many times in this book before, aim for 15 minutes a day.

For pre-verbal children, you can say the name of an animal or object, and encourage the child to point to the correct picture.

For toddlers who are starting to talk, encourage them to use words by asking lots of questions about the pictures: "Where's the horsey?" "What's Spot doing here?" "What colour is Pip's dress?"

One thing I'd like to point out is that when you read to your child, **try to sound as enthusiastic as possible, and use lots of dramatic facial expressions and gestures**; children respond to this "dramatic" style of reading a lot better and it's really beneficial for language acquisition. I know this sort of "acting" doesn't always come naturally to everyone, but the good thing is that your baby will *not* judge you so this is the perfect opportunity to discover your hidden acting talents!

Another trick is to deliberately make silly mistakes as you read. To use *Dear Zoo*, an English book as an example: instead of "I wrote to the zoo to send me a pet", you can say "I wrote to the *poo* to send me a pet" or "I wrote to the zoo to send me a *vet*". I guarantee your child will instantly pay attention to the story and will giggle with delight at your silly "mistakes"!

- **Play hide-and-seek with toys**

Give your child a toy and ask them to hide it. Count to 10, and you have to go find the toy. Then swap. Young children find this game incredibly entertaining and it's a great way to spend time at home on a rainy day. Incorporate lots of position words and prepositions into the game: "Is the dolly hiding *under* the table?" "I think the puppy is hiding *inside* the wardrobe!" This is such a fun game in itself but as a bonus your child will also be improving their language skills. And it's hilarious how a child thinks putting a teddy bear next to the chair right in front of your eyes counts as "hiding". Enjoy!

- **Play in a sandpit, either in your garden or in the park, ideally with some sand toys**

Most children *love* playing with sand. It also has the advantage of being one of the less messy "messy-play" activities as sand comes off easily once it's dry, which is great for mess-averse parents. It's a great way to incorporate lots of action words and prepositions, and your child will love exploring various textures and learning about physical properties of objects. Use lots of sentences like *"Use* the *spade* to *scoop* sand *into* the *bucket"* – the more varied the vocabulary, the better!

- **Get some paint and brushes out, or even just some crayons and pencils (for minimal mess) start drawing/ painting!**

Drawing and painting is a fantastic activity on so many levels – it helps children develop their fine motor skills, sense of colours and shapes, imagination, and an appreciation for beauty. When you draw or paint together, use lots of words related to colours and shapes to help them build their vocabulary. If you're painting, cut up some kitchen sponges to add interesting textures without having to buy any new equipment! Discarded cucumber and carrot bits can also be used as "stamps". And of course, your little one's hands (and even feet) make wonderful painting tools too!

- **Make playdough animals and objects**

You can use store-bought playdough, or make your own. Just Google "homemade playdough" for some recipes and make sure you get your child involved in all the mixing and kneading action! Your child will enjoy the physical sensations of manipulating playdough with their hands; home-made playdough in particular has a lovely squishy texture which is really quite addictive. Take this opportunity to expand your child's vocabulary in shapes, colours, names of animals and objects. Jazz up your works of art with toothpicks, pasta shapes or whatever else you have to hand.

- **Play with kitchen pantry staples such as pasta shapes, lentils and rice (or even flour, if you can handle the mess)**

Pour them into the largest bowl or pot you can find, give your child some spoons, ladles, cups or any other containers, and let them have some fun! You can pretend to measure things out, cook together, or even start a kitchen concert using wooden spatulas as drumsticks – just make sure to incorporate lots of action words and position words into your sentences to maximise the language-learning benefits.

2—5 years old

- **Cook or bake together**

Cooking and baking are fantastic ways to explore numbers, action words and position words. Let your child help you measure the various ingredients. If they can already recognise some numerals, they will relish the challenge of working out the number on the scales or measuring jug. If they're a bit younger, you can still count the number of spoonfuls of sugar/ squares of chocolate/ cups of water needed together. Let your child use a child-safe knife to help you cut up vegetables – any activity that hones their fine motor skills will set the foundation for learning to write later on. If your child is a fussy eater, cooking together is also known to help children develop healthier eating habits.

- **Cut out shapes or figures together and stick them onto a piece of paper or cardboard**

Most kids love sticking things, either using glue or just messing around with stickers. You can find cut-out pages in most children's magazines; alternatively, Google "kids cutout printout" and print some out at home. If your child is old enough to handle child-safe scissors, let them do the cutting themselves as it's great for developing their fine motor skills. Otherwise, you can do the cutting and they can do the sticking. Talk about the animals/ objects/ shapes of the cut-outs, and describe in detail how you use scissors to cut and how you use glue to stick the shapes on. Incorporate elements of imaginary play by recreating a "scene" on the cardboard using the cut-outs.

- **Play "guess which toy/ person/ cartoon character"**

One of you will choose a toy, cartoon character or a person you both know, and describe it/ her/ him verbally to the other person. The other person can ask questions and has to guess which toy/ person it is. This game is great for developing children's listening skills and descriptive vocabulary. It's also a great screen-free and equipment-free way to keep the kiddies occupied on long journeys.

- **Take "extreme close-ups" of a toy and let the other person guess which toy it is**

I got this idea from a children's magazine and it was a big hit with both of my kids! Some of our snapshots were genuinely hilarious and I still have them on my phone as "favourites". You'll both be surprised and amused by how dramatically different things can look when examined from an unusual angle!

- **Look at a world map or globe together, and talk about different places**

Make connections to people you know. Put stickers on places you've been to. This exercise is not only great for language learning but will stimulate your child's interest in the world.

- **Play "Spot-the-Difference"**

You can use specialised "Spot-the-Difference" books, or download worksheets from the internet. Most children's magazines also contain "Spot-the-Difference" exercises. This is a great way to incorporate lots of descriptive language, with the added benefit of improving your child's attention span and observational skills. Even as an adult, I find this to be a great "mindfulness" exercise!

- **Go on a "mission" in the park**

Assign tasks such as "collect 10 pine cones" or "see who will be the first to find a snail!" Language benefits aside, this is a great way for children to connect with nature and get some fresh air.

- **Look at family pictures together and talk about places and people in them**

This is a great language-learning as well as bonding exercise; talking about the past also helps your child develop a sense of time, narrative and imagination.

- **Make a card together**

You don't need a special occasion to get some paper, pens and scissors out! This is also a good opportunity to practise writing some simple words in the target language.

- **Build a house using some Amazon delivery boxes**

You do have one of those lying around, don't you? Draw on it, stick bits on it, wrap things around it... Get some toys out (figurines, soft toys, toy kitchen equipment, toy cars...) and enjoy some really fun role-play with your pretend house/ school/ shop/ train/ spaceship...

- **Find a funny or educational video in your target language on Youtube and watch it together**

I know some parents would not let their kids go near Youtube but personally I think that, like most things, Youtube can be beneficial in moderation. Obviously Youtube-time needs to be supervised but if you do it together it can be a good introduction to basic IT skills (finding Youtube on the browser; typing in various search words etc.), IT-related vocabulary in the target language, as well as input methods in your target language. While there are certainly too many rubbish kids' videos on Youtube that are quite simply toy or junk food advertisements in disguise, there's also lots and lots of genuinely engaging, educational content in a vast number of languages that's specifically aimed at children. The tool is there; it's up to you how you use it!

- **Play around with Google Translate**

You can even explore some new, random, exotic languages together!

School-age children

- **Have a popcorn-and-film night together**

Needless to say, the film should be in the target language. Discuss the storyline, the characters, how the film makes you feel – just as you would with any other person, but with the added benefit of practising the target language!

- **Read a newspaper article written in the target language**

Discuss news stories and talk about interesting images together. Apart from the language benefits, this is also a great introduction to the print media and current affairs for your school-age child. Grocery stores selling produce from the country where the target language is spoken are usually a good place to look for such newspapers. If you can't find any physical newspapers in the target language where you live, do have a look on Google for digital versions.

- **Giving instructions in the target language, direct your child to perform a task or a chore independently**

It can be washing dishes, hoovering, doing the laundry – just make sure they're supervised if any fragile objects are involved!

- **Play a version of "i spy with my little eye" in the target language**

Apart from language skills, this game is great for helping children develop their observational skills and improve their concentration. And it's a great screen-free, zero-cost way to keep the kids occupied anywhere.

- **Play "Describe the Difference"**

Name any two animals, objects or even abstract concepts and ask your child to describe their differences. Then swap. From a linguistic

111

perspective, this game is great for helping your child hone their descriptive skills in the target language; it also helps improve their general cognitive abilities. To make this activity more visual, prepare a set of cards (they can be made with just plain printed A4 paper) with images or just words. Each of you gets a set of cards and each reveals one card at the same time. Compare the differences between the two things shown on the cards.

- **Go on a "treasure hunt" in a museum**

Before visiting a museum, do some research together and identify interesting "treasures". Make a list of them and perhaps print out a map of the museum too. Once you're at the museum, tick those "treasures" off the list as you locate them! This creates a wonderful sense of adventure for children who may not always find museums all that interesting. When you need a break, make your way to the cafe for a well-deserved cappuccino and slice of cake…

Go to a restaurant (where the target language is spoken) and ask your child to order food in the target language

Okay, this may not be feasible for your target language, depending on what your target language is and where you live. But if you can find a suitable restaurant, it can be a great opportunity for your child to use their language skills in a novel setting, with people other than their parents. The food is a nice bonus too!

Some general advice

- One thing worth reiterating again and again is this: **every single interaction you or another caregiver has with your child in the target language will help them acquire the language in a natural way.** That means any age-appropriate activity that any parent – monolingual or otherwise – would normally do with a child could be beneficial for language-acquisition purposes. So, take the pressure off yourself a little – you don't have to "go all out" and get a dozen arts and crafts kits out, or spend a small fortune on sourcing hard-to-find materials, or the latest gadgets. **Just focus on spending quality time with your child, as much as your work and other commitments allow.**

- Some of the activities I suggested above are screen-based. Screen use for children is a controversial topic but in reality, children will have to learn to use electronic devices one day so if it can be used in a constructive, educational way, and it's done in a controlled, supervised setting, it *can* be a very useful tool. **The important thing to bear in mind is that to fully take advantage of digital media for the purposes of language acquisition, especially when young children are involved, a parent or caregiver should be present to supervise and provide interaction.** Ask questions about the cartoon you're watching together. Make funny comments on their favourite Youtube video. Giggle together about hilarious translations on Google Translate. Leaving a young child to their own devices (excuse the pun) with a phone or iPad for long stretches of time may sometimes be necessary as a "childcare" solution (almost every parent I know has been guilty of this at times, especially during the pandemic) but won't do much good in terms of language acquisition or indeed general development.

- For busy parents, finding time to do fun and educational activities with your kids during the week can sometimes feel like mission impossible. That's totally understandable. So if you and/or your partner work long hours during the week, it's okay to adjust your expectations. Don't feel like you have to somehow fit in 10 different activities in those two hours between dinner time and bedtime. As I said before, reading together is one of the most beneficial activities you can do with your child. So **if you have time for absolutely nothing**

else, make sure you still spend 15 minutes a day reading with your child. Sometimes, of course, life gets in the way and you really, really can't even squeeze in 15 minutes of reading time in the evening, with all the work and chores and what not... And that's okay. **Not every day will be perfect but just remember, every little bit counts and it will all add up in the long term**.

In his book, *Maximize your Child's Bilingual Ability*, Adam Beck made one point that struck a chord with me: while spending tons of time talking to your child and doing lots of different activities in the target language can, at times, feel like a chore, **every minute you spend with your child strengthens that precious parent-and-child bond** which is – I'm sure you'll agree – one of the most beautiful and treasured gifts in life. This is one simple point that's so easily overlooked in the daily grind of parenting. In retrospect, you'll find that those years just flew by and before you know it, they won't be demanding your attention all the time anymore and you'll probably miss those days when your child would bombard you with silly questions in their sweet, innocent way. Cherish every moment you spend with your child on this wonderful journey of parenthood.

Hopefully this chapter has given you some inspiration on how to help your child improve their language skills in a fun, engaging way. In the next chapter, I've put together a list of resources – from online language programmes to digital libraries – that multilingual families may find useful.

CHAPTER 9

USEFUL RESOURCES

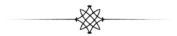

In this chapter, I've collated a compact list of useful resources for multilingual families. Compared to twenty years ago, resources are so much easier to come by, thanks to the Internet – in fact, the problem is often not too little information, but too much! Nonetheless, on balance, the Internet is such a fantastic tool not only for finding books, study materials, worksheets and the like, but perhaps even more importantly, for connecting with other families who are also trying to raise their children to speak more than one language. I hope some of the resources here will be of help to you.

An important disclaimer: all my comments below reflect my honest opinions on each resource. I have *not* been paid by anyone or any company, nor am I affiliated with any of them in any way.

Books

- *Maximize Your Child's Bilingual Ability: Ideas and inspiration for even greater success and joy raising bilingual kids* by Adam Beck

I've referred to this excellent book by Adam Beck many times throughtout this book. In my opinion this is one of the most accessible books on the subject, with lots of practical and motivational advice.

- *Be Bilingual - Practical Ideas for Multilingual Families* by Annika Bourgogne

A very accessible book on the subject, which does a great job balancing academic research (in sections titled "Words of the Wise") and practical ideas (in sections titled "View from the Frontline").

- *Trilingual by Six: The Sane way to raise intelligent, talented children* by Lennis Dippel MD

Some interesting insights and ideas, especially for trilingual families.

- *The Bilingual Edge, the: Why, When and How to Teach Your Child a Second Language* by Kendall King and Alison Mackey

- *7 Steps to Raising a Bilingual Child* by Naomi Steiner

Online language-learning programmes

- **Duolingo** (duolingo.com)

Duolingo is one of the most popular and well-known online language-learning programmes and it's 100% free! At the time of writing it offers courses in 37 languages including all the major modern languages, plus some pretty niche ones like Esperanto and Scottish Gaelic. It's mostly targeted at adult learners but the attractive interface and extensive use of cartoon characters will appeal to children too. Just a small caveat – it is primarily a text-based programme, which means your child would have to be able to at least read some basic words in the target language to benefit from Duolingo. The unique selling point of this programme is that each course is divided into manageable chunks and is designed based on the principle of spaced repetition. Just 10 minutes a day can really help you build your vocabulary.

- **Dinolingo** (dinolingo.com)

Dinolingo (not to be confused with *Duo*lingo!) is one of the largest online language-learning programmes for children, and is available in 50 languages. I subscribed to the Chinese programme for six months when they were running a special promotion (I paid the equivalent of approximately £10 a month) and found it to be one of the better programmes of its kind. The content is pretty good overall and most importantly, my kids enjoyed the videos and especially the games. Personally I found the graphics very dated but it didn't seem to bother my kids! Subscribers can also take advantage of the free Dinolingo smartphone app for easy access. The monthly subscription cost is currently $19.99 a month but make sure you sign up for the free trial first.

- **Muzzy BBC**   (muzzybbc.com)

Available in seven languages. It's similar to Dinolingo although, in my personal opinion, not quite as good. During my one-week free trial, I found the graphics and interface very dated, like something you'd expect from a software from the late nineties or early noughties. The games also felt somewhat repetitive. The good thing is that it's slightly cheaper than Dinolingo – a one-year subscription works out to be US$8.25 a month. Definitely sign up for a free trial before subscribing though.

- **Little Pim** (littlepim.com)

Available in 12 languages. I haven't tried this programme myself but according to their website, it is specifically aimed at younger children, ages 1—5. The programme is said to teach children 360 basic words in the target language, which should be an excellent starting point. Subscription starts from $9.99 a month.

- **FluentU** (fluentu.com)

I've been using FluentU to help improve my Russian and it's really exceeded my expectations. Initially I was slightly put off by the high subscription cost (which starts from $20/ month) but after a two-week free trial, I can really attest to how much effort the FluentU team have put into creating a truly user-friendly product, which combines authentic real-life materials (clips from real movies and music videos, for example) and language-learning functionalities (interactive subtitles with option to add new words to flashcards). This programme is geared towards adults but can also be useful for slightly older children – a lot of the videos are clips are from popular cartoons. I would highly recommend signing up for a free trial.

- **PetraLingua** (petralingua.com)

This learning programme is aimed at children aged 3—10, with a focus on vocabulary building. It offers courses in English, Spanish, Chinese, German and Russian. Each course includes around 500 basic words, 80 language-learning videos, 11 language-learning songs, 140 interactive online games and a talking picture dictionary. I haven't tried this programme myself but the relatively low subscription cost (from $3.99 a month) makes it an attractive option.

- **Languagenut** (languagenut.com)

Languagenut mostly offers digital language resources for primary and secondary schools, but a subscription option for individual users is also available. At primary-school level (both for schools and individual users) it gives subscribers access to 22 modern foreign languages including French, German, Spanish and Mandarin. Each course comprises 1,440 words and phrases, verb conjugation activities, interactive games and others features, all packaged in an attractive, modern user interface, complete with a mobile App. I haven't tried Languagenut myself but must admit that it looks like one of the better programmes of its kind. At the time of writing, a primary/elementary school subscription for individual users costs £19.95 per *year*, which is very competitive. No free trial is available though unfortunately.

118

Websites for multilingual families

- Chalkacademy.com

I discovered this website by chance while searching for Chinese materials for my children. Betty Choi, the founder of the website and a Harvard-trained pediatrician, is a truly inspirational figure especially for those parents who are raising their kids to be bilingual as non-fluent speakers of the target language themselves. The CHALK Academy website ("CHALK" stands for Child-Led, Hands-on, Active Learning for Kids) offers a wealth of resources for multilingual families, from practical tips to motivational articles. The actual learning materials are specific to Chinese and Korean, but on the website Betty Choi also shares lots of useful tips on raising bilingual/ multilingual children based on her own experience as a third-generation Chinese American who's not fluent in the language herself. I highly recommend visiting this website for some inspiration and practical advice.

- Bilingualfamily.eu

This website is the online platform for the PEaCH project, which stands for "Preserving and promoting Europe's cultural and linguistic heritage though empowerment of bilingual children and families" (you can see why an acronym is quite necessary!). In essence, the EU-sponsored project supports European families raising bilingual and multilingual children with ample resources, including a free downloadable handbook for parents, informative videos and an online collection of ready-to-use materials in all 24 EU languages. Definitely worth checking out.

- Bilingualmonkeys.com

A blog created by Adam Beck, the author of *Maximize Your Child's Bilingual Ability,* with lots of interesting articles and useful tips for bilingual families. Also features a forum called "The Bilingual Zoo" for families to connect and share their experiences and tips.

- Multilingualparenting.com

Here you'll find a substantial collection of articles covering a wide range of topic related to multilingual parenting, from family life to raising bilingual teenagers, all sorted by categories for easy navigation.

- Incultureparent.com

As a website dedicated to "parents raising little global citizens", InCultureParent has a strong focus on the cultural aspect of mixed-heritage parenting but if you're specifically looking for advice on bilingualism, the "Language" section of the website offers lots of useful information and interesting articles.

Other online resources

- International Children's Digital Library (en.childrenslibrary.org)

Throughout this book I've stressed the importance of reading for your child's linguistic development. If you struggle to source books in the target language, then this website could really come in handy! It's an online library of thousands of children's books, available in 18 languages including all the major European languages plus Chinese, Farsi, Mongolian and others. Although not all books are available in all 18 languages (in fact, there are only a measly *eight* books in Chinese!), it's still a fantastic resource for parents, especially considering it's *free*! You can filter books by language, age and theme (and even, quite randomly, the colour of the book cover), which makes it super easy to find a suitable book for your child. I highly recommend this website to all parents.

- Epic (getepic.com)

I discovered this website during the first lockdown in the UK last year. And honestly, I can say with absolute confidence that this is one of the *best* subscription services for families out there, and is worth every penny in my opinion. It's basically an online library of over 40,000 books and learning videos, all presented in a highly visually attractive interface. Kids can earn points and badges with every book they read, which is a great motivational feature – my children love checking their point status and genuinely want to read more books and complete quizzes to earn more badges. The best thing for multilingual families is that the website also offers a large number of books in languages including Spanish, Chinese and French! Subscribers can also download the excellent smartphone App and access the entire library everywhere you are. Subscription costs $7.99 a month after a one-month free trial. I have no intention to cancel our subscription any time soon – it truly is one of the best investments I've made!

- iTalki (italki.com)

Looking for the perfect language teacher? Look no further than iTalki, a fantastic platform for language learners who want to find the right language instructor. I discovered this website five years ago and found a wonderful Russian tutor from Azerbaijan with whom I had Skype lessons twice a week during my first pregnancy. As the teachers on this website come from all around the globe, you can often find teachers based in less expensive countries who charge very low rates by western standards. The booking system makes it all very simple and straightforward. If you'd like your child to have some extra one-on-one interaction in the target language, this could be a great option. If you're looking to improve your own proficiency in the target language, there's probably no better way to get low-cost, one-on-one lessons!

- The Mixxer (language-exchanges.org)

This free virtual language exchange site is designed to connect language learners around the world so that, as stated by the website, "everyone is both student and teacher". This website is great for older children, or for parents who want to brush up their own language skills!

- My Language Exchange (mylanguageexchange.com)

My Language Exchange prides itself on being "the only website with a proven language exchange method and lesson plans", which have been created by a qualified language teacher specialising in language-exchange learning. This should be perfect for those who want to benefit from language exchange in a more structured way.

- Global Pen Friends (globalpenfriends.com)

What better way to improve your language skills than by writing to a pen pal, either by email or – even better – by actual snail-mail? It's worth giving it a go just for the sake of reviving the lost art of letter-writing! Again, this is one for older children and possibly parents who want to improve their own language skills. You or your child may even meet some interesting people along the way.

NOTES FROM THE AUTHOR

Thank you so much for reading to the end of this book! I hope this little guide has given you some useful ideas on how to raise your child to speak more than one language, and helped you gain the confidence and motivation to embark on this wonderful journey. And language learning *is* a lifelong, ongoing journey – I really hope that you and your child will find speaking two or more languages in your daily life to be a rewarding and enriching experience.

If you've enjoyed this book, I'd be forever grateful if you could leave a review on Amazon, and recommend this book to someone who may benefit from it. If you have any questions, comments, feedback, or best of all, success stories, I'd love to hear from you!

Please visit my website The Multilingual Family Hub (www.multilingualfamilyhub.com), or email me at kayeejuliemeck@gmail.com.

ACKNOWLEDGEMENTS

Firstly, a big thanks to my friend and former student Mark Shanes, my fellow mum and personal cheerleader Stephanie Gordon, and my best friend and sister Florence Wong for reading an earlier draft of this book. Your encouragement, support and helpful feedback gave me the motivation to carry on!

A big shout out to Elisa Pinizzotto (Elisapinizzotto at Fiverr.com) for the lovely cover design.

Most of all, thank you to my husband Kirill for holding the fort in the evening and on the weekend to give me the time and space to work on this project. Without you, 24 hours a day would not have been enough!

ABOUT THE AUTHOR

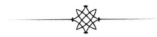

Ka Yee Meck is a freelance translator, language instructor and writer. She has an upper-second class BA Hons. Degree in History of Art from the University of Cambridge, and a Postgraduate Certificate in Teaching Chinese as a Foreign Language from SOAS (The School of Oriental and African Studies) in London. She currently lives in Watford, Hertfordshire with her husband, two children and their cat. Through this book and The Multilingual Family Hub website, she hopes to reach out to and help other families who wish to raise bilingual or multilingual children.

She's also the author of *Jade and Diamond*, a novel set in Hong Kong and London, available on Amazon.

Website: www.multilingualfamilyhub.com

Email: kayeejuliemeck@gmail.com

APPENDIX

GLOSSARY OF TERMS

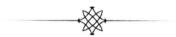

Bilingual: A person who is bilingual can fluently speak two languages.

Biliterate: A person who is biliterate can *read and write* proficiently in two languages. A person who is biliterate is also considered bilingual, but a person who is bilingual is not necessarily biliterate.

Community language: "Community languages" are languages spoken by members of minority groups or communities within a majority language context. However, somewhat confusingly, it is also used by some authors as a synonym for "majority language".

Conceptual vocabulary: a measure of a child's lexical knowledge in terms of the number of concepts he or she knows.

Expressive language: this refers to the "output" of language, the ability to express your thoughts and feelings through verbal or nonverbal communication.

Language acquisition device: a purported instinctive mental capacity that enables an infant to acquire and produce language

Majority language: A "majority language" is the language that's spoken by a majority of the population in a country or in a region of a country. In a multilingual society, the majority language is generally considered the high-status language.

Minority language: A "minority language" is a language spoken by a minority of the population of a territory.

Phoneme: A phoneme is the smallest unit of sound that distinguishes one word from another word in a language.

Receptive language: this refers to the "input" of language, the ability to understand and comprehend spoken or written language that you hear or read.

Scaffolding: Scaffolding refers to a variety of instructional techniques used to move students progressively toward stronger understanding and, ultimately, greater independence in the learning process.

Target language: A target language is a language other than one's native language that is being learned. In the context of translation, the target language is the language into which another language is to be translated.

Total vocabulary: the sum of the words a child knows across all his or her languages.

ENDNOTES

[i] Adani, S., & Cepanec, M. (2019). Sex differences in early communication development: behavioral and neurobiological indicators of more vulnerable communication system development in boys. *Croatian medical journal*, *60*(2), 141–149. https://doi.org/10.3325/cmj.2019.60.141

[ii] Dai, X., & Heckman, J. J. (2013). Older Siblings' Contributions to Young Child's Cognitive Skills. *Economic modelling*, *35*, 235–248. https://doi.org/10.1016/j.econmod.2013.07.003

[iii] Tailor, L. (July 10, 2019) How Howie Dorough's Identity Struggles Influenced His New Album "Which One Am I?" (Exclusive), *Etononline.com*. https://www.etonline.com/how-howie-doroughs-identity-struggles-influenced-his-new-album-which-one-am-i-exclusive-128188

[iv] Vince, G. (August 12, 2016) The amazing benefits of being bilingual, *BBC.com*. https://www.bbc.com/future/article/20160811-the-amazing-benefits-of-being-bilingual

[v] Abutalebi, J., Cappa S. F. & Perani, D. (August 2001) Bilingualism: Language and Cognition, Volume 4, Issue 2 , pp. 179 - 190

vi Bilingualism delays onset of dementia (12 January 2007) *Newscientist.com*. https://www.newscientist.com/article/dn10954-bilingualism-delays-onset-of-dementia/

vii Johnson: What is a foreign language worth? (11 March 2014) *Economist.com*. https://www.economist.com/prospero/2014/03/11/johnson-what-is-a-foreign-language-worth

viii University of Haifa. (2011, February 1). Bilinguals find it easier to learn a third language. *ScienceDaily*. Retrieved July 28, 2021 from www.sciencedaily.com/releases/2011/02/110201110915.htm

ix Marx, V. & Nagy, E. (2015) Fetal Behavioural Responses to Maternal Voice and Touch, DOI: 10.1371/journal.pone.0129118

x McElroy, M. (January 2, 2013) While in womb, babies begin learning languagee from their mothers, *University of Washington*. https://www.washington.edu/news/2013/01/02/while-in-womb-babies-begin-learning-language-from-their-mothers/

xi Marno, H., Guellai, B., Vidal, Y., Franzoi, J., Nespor, M. & Mehler, J. (2016) Infants Selectively Pay Attention to the Information They Receive from a Native Speaker of Their Language, *Frontiers in Psychology* 7:1150

xii Smith, D. G. (4 May 2018) At What Age Does Our Ability to Learn a New Language Like a Native Speaker Disappear? *Scientific American.com* https://www.scientificamerican.com/article/at-what-age-does-our-ability-to-learn-a-new-language-like-a-native-speaker-disappear/

[xiii] Bond, A. (12 March 2014) Kids with family routine more emotionally, socially advanced, *Reuters Health.* https://www.reuters.com/article/us-kids-family-routine-idUSBREA2B1TM20140312

[xiv] Ampel, B. C., Muraven, M., & McNay, E. C. (2018). Mental Work Requires Physical Energy: Self-Control Is Neither Exception nor Exceptional. *Frontiers in psychology, 9,* 1005. https://doi.org/10.3389/fpsyg.2018.01005

[xv] " 扫 除 文 盲 工 作 条 例 " (1993) ， http://www.humanrights.cn/html/2014/1_0812/1631.html

[xvi]https://www.bbc.co.uk/languages/chinese/real_chinese/mini_guides/characters/characters_howmany.shtml#:~:text=An%20educated%20Chinese%20person%20will,write%2060%20commonly%20used%20characters.

[xvii] De Houwer, A. (2007). Parental Language Input Patterns and Children's Bilingual Use. *Applied Psycholinguistics*, 28, 3, 411–424. DOI: 10.1017.S0142716407070221

[xviii] Making health habitual: the psychology of "habit-formation" and general practice, *British Journal of General Practice* 2012 Dec; 62(605): 664–666. DOI: 10.3399/bjgp12X659466

[xix] Byers-Heinlein K. & Lew-WilliamsC. (2013). Bilingualism in the Early Years: What the Science Says. *LEARNing Landscapes*, 7(1), 95-112. https://doi.org/10.36510/learnland.v7i1.632

[xx] Core, C., Hoff, E., Rumiche, R., & Señor, M. (2013). Total and conceptual vocabulary in Spanish-English bilinguals from 22 to 30 months: implications for assessment. *Journal of speech, language, and hearing research: JSLHR*, 56(5), 1637–1649. https://doi.org/10.1044/1092-4388(2013/11-0044)

[xxi] Treffers-Daller, J. and Milton, J. (2013) Vocabulary size revisited: the link between vocabulary size and academic achievement. *Applied Linguistics Review*, 4 (1). pp. 151-172. ISSN 1868-6311 DOI: https://doi.org/10.1515/applirev-2013- 0007 Available at http://centaur.reading.ac.uk/29879/

[xxii] Hoff, E., & Core, C. (2015). What Clinicians Need to Know about Bilingual Development. *Seminars in speech and language*, 36(2), 89–99. https://doi.org/10.1055/s-0035-1549104

[xxiii] Adescope, O.O., Lavin, T., and Thompson, T. *A Systematic Review and Meta-Analysis of the Cognitive Correlates of Bilingualism*. Review of Educational Research, June 2010, 80(2).

[xxiv] Byers-Heinlein, K., & Lew-Williams, C. (2013). Bilingualism in the Early Years: What the Science Says. *LEARNing landscapes*, 7(1), 95–112.

[xxv] Fernald, A. (1985), Four-month-old infants prefer to listen to motherese. *Infant Behavior and Development*, Volume 8, Issue 2, April-June 1985, pp. 181-195

Printed in Great Britain
by Amazon

83539642R00078